A GUIDE TO CAREERS WITH HORSES

By the same author

JUDGING HORSES AND PONIES (Pelham Books)
NEW FOREST PONIES (David & Charles)
DISCOVERING BRITISH PONIES (Shire Publications)

PELHAM HORSEMASTER SERIES

A GUIDE TO CAREERS WITH HORSES

Valerie Russell

Valerie Russell

PELHAM BOOKS

First published in Great Britain by
PELHAM BOOKS LTD
44 Bedford Square
London WC1B 3DU
1980

ISBN 0 7207 1280 7

Typeset by Cambrian Typesetters, Farnborough
Printed in Great Britian by
Hollen Street Press, Slough
and bound by
Hunter and Foulis, Edinburgh

In memory of my mother

CONTENTS

ACKNOWLEDGEMENTS

A book of this kind cannot be written without generous assistance from official bodies and from individuals, who have supplied material and checked a number of the chapters for accuracy. I would like to thank most sincerely the following authorities for their help and, where appropriate, for allowing me to quote from their syllabuses: The British Horse Society, The Association of British Riding Schools, The National Pony Society, The British Show Jumping Association, The Jockey Club, The National Trainers' Federation, The Royal College of Veterinary Surgeons, The Household Cavalry, The King's Troop, Royal Horse Artillery, The Metropolitan Police (Mounted Branch), The Cordwainers' College, The Society of Master Saddlers, The Worshipful Company of Farriers, The Herefordshire Technical College (Engineering Department), The West Oxfordshire Technical College, The Warwickshire College of Agriculture, The University College of Wales at Aberystwyth, The Council for Small Industries in Rural Areas, The National Master Farriers', Blacksmiths' and Agricultural Engineers' Association, The Pony Trekking Society of Wales, The English Riding Holiday and Trekking Association, The Scottish Trekking and Riding Association, and The Master of Foxhounds Association. My grateful thanks to the following individuals: Mrs Molly Sivewright, FBHS, Lt.Col. J.D. Crawford, FBHS, Mrs M. Simlo, Mrs Pauline Harris, Mrs R.M. Taylor, Lt.Col. P. Heaton-Ellis, RA, The Commanding Officer, The Household Cavalry, Hyde Park Barracks, Capt. N. Hadden-Paton, Capt. N.M. Cowdery, RHA, Mr I. Forbes-Cockell, Major (Ret'd) R.A.G. Courage, MVO, MBE, Major R.C. Wilkinson, Inspector R. Jordan, Mrs Jane Blizzard, Mrs Diana Keal, Mr Harry Douglas, FABRS, FBHS, Mr P.M. Roberts, Mrs L. Holder, Mr J. Onions, Mr J. Arthur George,

DBHS, Mr J. Gilbert, Mrs Y. Learmouth, Miss Angela Heaton, Lt.Cdr. W.B. Jeffries, Miss E. Dixon, Mr R.D. Britter, Mr J.L. Lees, Mr A.H.B. Hart, Mr Dickens.

INTRODUCTION

It is perhaps something of a cliché to say that working with horses is not so much a career as a way of life. The purpose of this book is to show that in many instances it can be both, while at the same time pointing out the difficulties and disadvantages as well as the pleasures of a life with horses.

One of the most striking features of careers with horses is that there is such a wide range — from careers in which the horse and its activities are the sole focus of attention, to others, such as the Army or the Mounted Police, where the horse is a part, albeit an important part, of a career with many other facets. There are opportunities for those with ambitions to own their own businesses — perhaps a riding school, training centre, or trekking establishment — and for those who want to exploit their manual dexterity in such skills as saddlery or farriery. Of more recent origin are the courses in colleges of higher education that appeal to the academically inclined with the wish and ability to learn more of the theory behind horses and their activities, as well as the practical side. Those with the ability to teach can combine that with their love of horses, as instructors.

There is an infinite variety, but the people who choose to work with horses must have at least one thing in common — complete dedication to the animals. Anyone who is not prepared to put the horses first, however inconvenient or tiring that may be at times, really should look for a career elsewhere. The hours of work, as will be stressed time and again in the following chapters, are very long, and the work itself frequently physically demanding. Financial rewards are, on the whole, in no way commensurate with the time and effort expended. But, for the genuine lover of horses, the disadvantages and difficulties are there to be overcome, and the satisfaction and pleasure to be gained make it well worth while.

On a more practical note, young people with ambitions to make a career with horses should make a serious effort to find out just what this entails before finally committing themselves. Holidays or weekends spent helping in the local riding school, stud, or livery stables are the most obvious way, and owners are, on the whole, sympathetic and helpful to young people who are keen to do this.

It was intended to include in the following chapters some details of the various grants etc. available for people wishing to train for qualifications in the horse world. However, at the time of writing, with so many authorities making economies, such information is likely to be out of date almost before it is written. Anyone hoping for a grant or financial assistance should consult their local authority, the body whose qualifications he or she hopes to acquire, or a school careers officer, to gain the latest details.

Included in some of the chapters are detailed descriptions of syllabuses and/or examinations. Readers who are not interested in those particular careers may find this tedious, but I believe they serve an important function in assisting prospective students to choose the most suitable course for their purpose. So often it is only by reading the syllabus or knowing the type of exercises set in examinations that the aim and emphasis of a course can be appreciated fully.

1 Instructing

For those who combine a love of horses and riding with the ability to pass on their knowledge to others, instructing offers a worthwhile and rewarding career. Intending instructors must have the gift of truly understanding the natural nervousness of beginners, and of inspiring confidence in riders at all levels. They must also have a genuine interest in people (as well as horses!) and possess the patience and enthusiasm to bring out the best in all their pupils, especially those with little ability whose progress may sometimes seem agonisingly slow. But for people with these qualities there is the enormous satisfaction of seeing, for example, a tense, nervous rider gradually relax, gain confidence and skill, and begin to form a partnership with a horse or pony. At the more advanced levels of teaching there is the great challenge of preparing riders for higher examinations or for competitive riding.

Not least among the attractions of instructing is the opportunity it can offer of working not only in different parts of Britain, but of obtaining positions in many countries overseas where British-trained instructors are in demand. The really ambitious will aim at becoming chief instructors or principals, or, possibly, owning their own riding school or training establishment.

Irrespective of the level at which they plan to teach, the possession of a recognised qualification is almost essential. The British Horse Society conducts a series of examinations for certificates which, while primarily designed for instructors, also provide evidence for prospective employers in all branches of the horse world that the holder has reached certain standards in riding and general horsemastership. The certificates are, in ascending order, the British Horse Society's Assistant

Instructor's, the BHS Intermediate Instructor's, the BHS Instructor's, and the Fellowship of the BHS.

The most basic of these, the BHS Assistant Instructor's, is the very first rung on the instructional ladder, and should not be regarded as a full professional qualification; that status should be accorded only to holders of the BHS Instructor's Certificate and Fellows of the BHS. As its name suggests, it is evidence that the holder is considered competent to be an *assistant* instructor (or assistant in any other type of stable) and it should be appreciated that its holders are, in most instances, just at the beginning of their careers and still have much to learn.

Candidates for the BHS Assistant Instructor's Certificate must have reached the age of seventeen and a half years, be members of the BHS and (unless they are over twenty years of age) are expected to hold four GCE 'O' level passes at Grade C or above, or CSE Grade 1, including either English language or literature. Certain examinations passed by overseas candidates are accepted as equivalent to these passes.

With the aim of improving the instructional standard of the BHS Assistant Instructor's Certificate, the BHS is introducing, from 1st January 1981, a new syllabus for the examination. It is to be in two parts, the first of which, the BHS Certificate of Horsemastership, will be awarded to candidates who pass in:

1. Equitation;
2. Stable management;
3. Minor ailments (a forty-five-minute written paper);
4. Riding and leading and/or lungeing.

The second part, held on a separate day, is the BHS Preliminary Teaching Test in which candidates are examined on the four basic subjects described in the syllabus below. In order to obtain the BHS Assistant Instructor's Certificate, candidates must pass both the Preliminary Teaching Test and the Certificate of Horsemastership, although they need not be taken at the same time. However, they must be taken within three years of each other to qualify. For candidates who have no intention of teaching, but who want certificated evidence of competence, the BHS Certificate of Horsemastership may be taken on its own. The educational requirements for admission to the BHS Assistant Instructor's Certificate do not apply to candidates who plan to take the Certificate of Horsemastership *only,* but if such candidates subsequently decide to take the Preliminary Teaching Test in order to obtain the BHS Assistant Instructor's Certificate, they must, if under twenty, comply with the educational requirements.

Details of the syllabus for the BHS Assistant Instructor's Certificate are as follows:

Certificate of Horsemastership

1.   *Equitation.* Candidates will be examined for their riding in the open and/or in a covered school. Candidates must have:

(*a*)   A good seat and position and the ability to apply the aids correctly.

(*b*)   A knowledge of the correct basic paces of the horse.

(*c*)   The ability to ride simple school movements (turns, circles, changes of pace and directions, etc.).

(*d*)   The ability to jump fences up to 3 feet in good style and with fluency, from trot and canter. The course will include doubles and changes of direction.

2.   *Stable management and horsemastership.* Candidates must show a sound practical knowledge of how to handle horses and of:

(*a*)   Stable routine: daily programme — feeding, watering, bedding, mucking out, sweeping, etc.; care and cleanliness of tack room, feed shed, muck heap, etc.; care and use of all grooming kit and horse clothing.

(*b*)   Care of stabled horses: feeding, watering, grooming, rugging, bandaging, exercise, recognition of lameness or ill health, preparing horses for a journey, care while travelling, care of hunters and competition horses, reason

for clipping, how to clip, types of clip, singeing, plaiting
and trimming (manes, heels, etc.).

(c)   Care of horses at grass: suitability of area — terrain,
watering, fencing, shelter, poisonous plants, etc. Supervision of horses — feeding, health, warmth, settling with
others, inspection for wounds or sores, protection from
flies. How to prepare horses to be turned out or got up
from grass.

(d)   Saddlery: all types of saddlery in common use, with
their respective advantages and disadvantages (saddles,
bridles, bits, head collars, boots, etc.); fitting, checking
and care of saddlery. Precautions against injuries (sore
backs, galls, etc.).

(e)   Shoeing: conformation of the foot and care of feet;
reasons for shoeing; recognition of well or badly shod or
neglected feet; reasons for special shoeing; shoeing tools
and procedures; how to remove a shoe.

(f)   Conformation; basic knowledge of structure of the
horse; points of the horse; types and markings. Points + pony

3.   *Minor ailments.* Written paper; normally five questions in forty-five minutes covering: A - Z of ailments.

(a)   Elementary rules of nursing a sick horse. Signs of
good or ill health. How to take temperature, pulse and
respiration.

(b)   How to deal with infection and contagion (coughs,
colds, flu, strangles, fever, skin diseases, etc.).

(c)   How to dress wounds, clean cuts, tears, punctures,
contusions, galls, sprains, broken knees, etc.; how to tub,
foment, poultice and hose. Knowledge of first aid in an
emergency, how to deal with excessive bleeding, shock,
colic, azoturia, etc. H of Pony.

(d)   Signs of unsoundness — feet, limbs and wind and
how to diagnose the seat of lameness.

(e)   Administration of medicines and the advantages
and disadvantages of various methods.

(f)   When to call the veterinary surgeon and what information to give.

4.   *Ride and lead and/or lunge*

Preliminary teaching test

Candidates must show that they have the required abilities, and can apply the basic principles of teaching, such as manner, voice, control, etc., and that they have the ability to improve their pupil's horsemanship and horsemastership with a progressive plan. They must know the procedure and principles with regard to safety in the stage management of a lesson or hack. They must have knowledge of how to proceed should there be an accident or an emergency, and have knowledge of road safety. Candidates will be examined in their ability to:

1.　Give a leading-rein lesson suitable for a complete beginner, or give a lunge lesson suitable for a novice adult or child rider. Instructor's handbook.

2.　Take a lesson of three or four pupils, showing a sound knowledge of basic equitation.

3.　Take a lesson of two to four pupils, working over ground-poles or cavelletti, and/or give an early jumping lesson. Instructors handbook.

4(a).　Give stable management oral/practical lecturettes of three to five minutes suitable for Horse Knowledge and Riding Stage II, Riding Clubs Grade II, Pony Club 'C' Test standard pupils.

4(b).　Answer simple questions on safety, accident procedure, basic equitation and stable management principles. (Candidates may be required to give these lessons in the open and/or a covered school.)

A typical examination for the Certificate of Horsemastership begins with the equitation section, which lasts for up to an hour. Candidates are examined in groups of four or five, and at intervals during the test are required to change horses so that the examiners can assess their ability to adapt to different animals. Normally, they are seen riding out of doors as well as inside if the centre has a covered school. The required exercises are commanded from the centre of the manège, and each candidate is asked to perform individually. They will be required to walk, trot and canter with and without stirrups, so that the examiners can judge their control, position, transitions and general ability. Subsequent exercises may include turns on the forehand, a rein back, changes of diagonals, a few lengthened strides, a simple exercise with the reins held in one hand and figures of eight with simple changes. Each candidate is then required to ride at least two horses over a small course of fences, which include a double and one or more changes of rein. The examiners look particularly for fluent harmony, coupled with a strong, independent seat. Lack of these qualities is probably the single most common cause of failure in the equitation section.

The written paper on minor ailments typically contains five short, straightforward questions, for example, 'Name three parasites of the horse. Give the symptoms and treatment for dealing with one of them.'

Stable management is examined in three sections: oral, practical, and practical oral. The practical section involves such tests as plaiting part of a mane, demonstrating grooming techniques, putting on various types of bandages, fitting a double bridle, putting on a saddle and commenting on its fit, or rugging up.

One examiner takes a group of three or four candidates for the oral examination, lasting forty or forty-five minutes, during which they are questioned on a variety of topics and are required to comment on or add to the answers given by their colleagues. Questions discussed in a recent examination included 'What are the rules for feeding stabled horses? How would you feed the average 16-hand hunter? At the end of the hunting season how would you let down and turn out a hunter? What would you do if you were put in charge of a tack room?' Candidates may also be asked to identify and comment on, for instance, different samples of foodstuffs, or a selection of bits.

In the practical oral section, candidates might be taken into a stable block and asked to comment on its good and bad points, and questioned on the design of the ideal stable; they could be questioned on the different types of bedding and their reasons for individual preferences; they might be faced with various grooming implements and asked to talk about them. Other topics could include commenting on the conformation of an individual horse or pony, on shoeing or on clipping.

Throughout the entire examination the examiners assess not only the practical ability and theoretical knowledge of the candidates, but also their approach and methods of handling the horses. It should be noted that the examiners are never dogmatic in their judgement of the candidate's methods. Their criteria is always 'Is it safe? Does it work?' An alternative method or answer will be accepted provided it falls within these criteria, and the candidate can offer a satisfactory reason for it.

The syllabus for the Preliminary Teaching Test is more or less self-explanatory, but there are a few points that perhaps need amplification in terms of what may actually be asked during the examination. In giving a leading-rein lesson to a complete beginner, the examiners expect the candidate to behave *exactly* as if the rider has never been on a horse before. They look, for example, for the candidate to start by showing the rider how to make friends with the horse or pony, how to mount correctly, and once mounted, how to sit and how to obtain extra security by holding the mane or neck-strap. During the class lesson, candidates will be asked to instruct on a particular subject, for example, turns on the forehand, transitions up and down from trot to canter, tightening the girths, shortening the reins, and improving their pupil's position and horsemanship. The examiners take note of candidates' voices, their control over the ride and their manner. The last of these is very important, and even in the short time of the examination, lack of patience and understanding can become readily apparent. The safety of the pupil is, of course, of paramount importance, and the examiners take the candidate's attention to this very much into consideration in their final assessment. They are, for instance, unlikely to be impressed by a candidate who gives a jumping lesson over fences that have unused cups and pins left on the stands.

Candidates are graded on each section of the two Certificates as 'pass', 'borderline pass', or 'fail'. The chief examiner moves from group to group throughout the examination, paying particular attention to those who are borderline. At the conclusion of the examination, examiners consider their assessments, and then invite the candidates in to hear the results. Each is given his or her results in the terms used above. After the formal announcements, candidates are able to talk to all the examiners and obtain brief individual assessments, with reasons for failure or for just achieving a borderline pass. The overall pass rate in the BHS Assistant Instructor's examination is approximately 50 per cent of candidates.

There are several different methods of preparing for the BHS Assistant Instructor's examination. The two most common are to attend as a full-time pupil (resident or non-resident) at one of the many riding schools offering courses, or to obtain a position as a working pupil in a riding school, or, perhaps less commonly, in a private stable. It is not absolutely necessary (although it is probably advisable) to attend a course of instruction, and more mature candidates sometimes rely successfully on their years of experience with horses as adequate preparation. The BHS publishes a booklet *Where to Ride* obtainable from the Society at the British Equestrian Centre, Stoneleigh, Kenilworth, Warwickshire, CV8 2LR, which lists all BHS-approved establishments and gives full details of those where students can train. It is not, however, obligatory to attend an approved establishment.

Full-time courses are usually of three to six months duration, depending on the school selected and, of course, on the previous knowledge and experience of the student. It is always advisable for prospective students to visit the establishment (or preferably a number of establishments) before making a final decision on where to train.

There are a large number of schools offering tuition, and as a result, there is some variation in the way courses are conducted. Most, however, ensure that students acquire a sound practical knowledge of stable management and horsemastership by allocating to them one or more horses to look after, much as might be done in subsequent employment. The student is responsible (under supervision) for these animals and attends to all their needs — grooming, feeding, tack cleaning, etc. In addition, practical and theoretical instruction is given in equitation, minor ailments, and all other topics on the syllabus. A number of schools take their students on educational visits to a variety of equestrian establishments such as veterinary research centres, studs, racing stables, etc., to widen their horizons and give them some idea of the types of work available if they decide to follow a career other than teaching.

Full-time courses can be quite expensive, particularly if students have been unable to obtain grants, so a number find it to their advantage to become working pupils. Arrangements for these vary widely, but in general, the pupil undertakes to work for the school or stable (usually for a predetermined period) in return for tuition and/or board and lodging, and occasionally for a small wage. The employer undertakes to prepare the pupil for the examination. The average working pupil can expect to take rather longer preparing for the examination because of the obligation to fit in the required number of hours working, instead of being able to devote all the time to studying and receiving tuition. There are no standard conditions (working hours, rates of pay, holidays, hours of tuition to be received, etc.) for working pupils, and there have been (and almost certainly still are) cases of exploitation. It is therefore advisable for the pupil to obtain a written contract (preferably drawn up by a solicitor) setting out clearly what is offered and expected from both sides. This advice also applies to working pupils preparing for the Association of British Riding Schools and the National Pony Society examinations which are discussed fully in later chapters.

Having obtained the BHS Assistant Inspector's Certificate, the next step in the prospective instructor's career is, of course, to obtain a suitable position. A number are advertised in the various horse magazines, and others may be obtained through personal contact or recommendation. By this time the student will probably have decided whether he or she *really* wants to make a career of teaching, or whether a change of direction is indicated. In either case, it is vital that great care is taken in the choice of a first position. Both employers *and* potential employees can fall into the trap of being too ambitious. At the risk of tedious repetition, it cannot be emphasised too strongly that (with the exception of certain mature students who have taken this first examination after years of working with horses) new BHS Assistant Instructors are young and relatively inexperienced. They should not, therefore, expect to walk straight into a 'high-powered' job as a senior instructor, and would be much better advised to start at the bottom as an assistant, while gaining valuable experience. Similarly, an employer must not expect too much. The possession of the Assistant Instructor's Certificate, while indicating the *potential* to go on to higher things, does not (without further experience) qualify the holder to be left in charge of a yard full of horses, or to give lessons in anything but relatively basic equitation or horsemastership without supervision.

Having definitely decided on an instructing career, the new Assistant Instructor will no doubt look forward to obtaining higher qualifications. The next step on the examination ladder is the BHS Intermediate Instructor's Certificate, followed by the final BHS Instructor's Certificate; the latter examination cannot be taken until the candidate is twenty-two years old. Study of the syllabus for these examinations shows that not only is considerable teaching experience required, but a wide knowledge and practical experience of training horses, and a much higher standard of riding than is accepted for the Assistant Instructor's Certificate.

How best to achieve the necessary standards must surely influence the type of employment that the young instructor will seek during the next few years. Clearly, as much experience as possible over a wide range is imperative, and this may be gained in a number of different ways. Initially, further teaching experience, perhaps as a junior in a reasonably large establishment, might be advisable. In this situation there is always the possibility of receiving further instruction from senior staff members, and helping with schooling for various events if the school has competition horses. Some may prefer to work in a smaller school with perhaps a little more responsibility and the chance of working more closely with the proprietor and thus learning about the essential business of organising and running a yard. This would be particularly valuable for anyone with ambitions to own their own school in due course. Later on, the young instructor might leave teaching for a time, and work in a stable that specialises in training horses for dressage, show jumping or eventing, bearing in mind that BHS Instructor candidates must be capable of both riding and teaching to Medium standard in dressage, Grade C in show jumping, and horse trials. A period spent working in a stud would provide the necessary background for the Stable Manager's Certificate section of the Instructor's Certificate on the care of mares and foals and young stock.

An infinite variety of jobs *is* available, and most experience can be put to good use in preparing for higher qualification. There is no real substitute for actual working experience, but a number of candidates for the BHS Intermediate and the BHS Instructor's Certificates feel that a further course of tuition specifically aimed at these certificates will give them added confidence. Courses are available (albeit much less readily than for the Assistant Instructor's Certificate) at most of the leading BHS establishments.

To qualify for the Intermediate Instructor's Certificate, candidates must hold the BHS Assistant Instructor's Certificate, and are then required to pass the Intermediate Teaching Certificate together with any *one* of the following:

(a)   the BHS Horse Knowledge and Riding, Stage IV;
(b)   the Riding Clubs' Grade IV;
(c)   the Pony Club 'A' Test.

The full BHS Instructor's examination consists of three separate certificates: the BHS Equitation, the BHS Teaching, and the BHS Stable Manager; these may be taken together or separately. Anyone entering the full examination must already hold the BHS Intermediate Instructor's Certificate.

The really ambitious instructor will in due course want to try for the Fellowship of the BHS. This is open to BHS members who have reached their twenty-fifth birthday, and are holders of the BHS Instructor's Certificate and/or the Fellowship of the Institute of the Horse. They must also produce evidence of having two years' practical instructing during the previous five. As might be expected, a depth of knowledge as well as a high standard in all branches of horsemanship, equitation, and horsemastership are demanded. But the examination requires even more than that, as befits aspirants to the British Horse Society's highest qualification. They must be capable of chairing a meeting and show that they are people to whom others can turn for advice in the various spheres of equestrian activities. They must also be familiar with all BHS publications and well-known books dealing with horses, so that they can discuss with clarity equestrian history, the various international schools and current trends and controversies in equitation. That fewer than fifty people have been awarded their Fellowship since 1949 underlines the challenge the examination presents — but for the person aiming at the top in instructing, it must surely be the ultimate aim.

Throughout this chapter it has, to a large extent, been assumed that people taking the various BHS instructors' examinations *do* intend to teach. Later chapters, however, show that the possession of these qualifications frequently provides the means of entry into an extremely wide range of other equestrian activities.

Further information, together with copies of the syllabuses for all BHS examinations may be obtained from the British Horse Society at Stoneleigh.

2 Training as a Groom

A glance through the 'Situations Vacant' columns of horse magazines leaves little doubt that there is a widespread demand for grooms in an almost infinite variety of stables both in Britain and overseas. To the real horse lover, the enjoyment and satisfaction obtained from looking after the day-to-day needs of the animals and turning them out in tiptop condition more than compensates for the hard work and long and freqently unsocial hours.

Until comparatively recently, however, there was no professional qualification exclusively for grooms that could give employers any indication of the standard of a prospective employee. In 1967, however, the Association of British Riding Schools introduced its Grooms' Diploma examination, and this has very quickly gained wide recognition and respect. It differs from the BHS Assistant Instructor's Certificate in three important ways: it is not a teaching qualification; it can only be taken by candidates who produce evidence of at least eighteen months in full-time occupation with horses and, possibly most important of all, it is not an assistant's qualification — it is awarded to candidates whom the examiners consider capable of working without supervision and who could safely be left in charge during an owner's absence.

The ABRS stress that although the examination is open to candidates who have reached the age of eighteen years, it is primarily designed for those who have a wide experience and knowledge of horses, and a very high standard indeed is expected. The pass rate of thirty per cent underlines this. Nevertheless, this should not discourage entry for the examination, as it really is a worthwhile qualification. Candidates who just fail to reach the full Grooms' Diploma standard and whom the examiners feel still require supervision in employment are awarded the Assistant Grooms' Certificate, and are encouraged to take the examination again when they have gained further experience.

The examination is a practical and oral one, covering the care of fit, stabled horses, and candidates, being competent in all stable duties, must show their ability to adapt their knowledge and experience to specialised work such as hunters, competitive horses, polo ponies, show horses and ponies, etc. The actual syllabus is as follows:

Daily routine — to establish a daily routine to include mucking out and bedding down. Grooming, clipping, trimming, mane and tail pulling and plaiting, rugging and bandaging. Complete preparation for a journey.
Saddlery — care and cleaning, fitting and uses of saddlery.
Shoeing — recognise worn or ill-fitting shoes and demonstrate ability to remove broken or twisted shoes, show knowledge of simple corrective and surgical shoes.
Feeding — candidates must show, in their knowledge of feeding, the ability to adapt to requirements for specialised work.
Veterinary — health routine, worming, vaccination, fomenting, hosing, poulticing, care of sick horses, taking temperature and pulse, dressing and treating of wounds.
Riding — candidates must show they are practical horsemen, capable of exercising a fit clipped horse in the open and able to jump small natural fences. Be able to ride and lead fit horses. Have a knowledge of the Highway Code.
Lungeing — to be capable of exercising and working a fit horse on the lunge.
Management — show knowledge of care of pasture and general maintenance of establishment.
Administration — to establish a daily routine which will include knowledge of records to be kept. Fire drill. Control and instructions to junior staff.

General — examiners will take into consideration the candidates' manner in handling horses, also their general approach and tidiness in their work, including mode of dress.

The examination takes place over two days, beginning at 2 p.m. on the first day and ending between 4 p.m. and 4.30 p.m. on the second. Before the start of the actual examination, candidates are welcomed by the chief examiner and taken on a tour of inspection of the centre so that they know where everything is, and they are introduced to their allotted horses. The chief examiner also gives them a friendly briefing, to which particular attention should be paid, as from this candidates can learn much about the examiners' expectations. They will be told, for instance, that they should approach their horse and stable *exactly* as if they were just taking up a new post. The chief examiner will almost certainly emphasise that candidates should perform their given tasks precisely as they would under working conditions, and remarks such as 'If I was really doing this I would do such and such' are totally unacceptable.

After the initial briefing, candidates are examined practically and orally on lungeing, various tasks such as plaiting, preparing the horse for a journey, and putting down night beds. For the lungeing test, the grooms are told that for some reason the horse, which is hunting fit, cannot be ridden and therefore needs compensating work on the lunge. The examiners expect, of course, that candidates should be able to handle the lungeing equipment correctly, but they also want to see a planned routine of useful work for the horse. They *do not* want to see a horse being allowed to amble aimlessly around doing little or no real work, but neither do they want to see a spectacular whip-cracking display with a 'hotted-up' horse and the accompanying possibility of ruining it for lungeing or laming it. At all stages the examiners are looking for a person they themselves would feel confident of leaving in charge of their own horses.

On the second day, candidates are asked to demonstrate their familiarity with stable routine. In the morning, they are told that their horses have been fed and watered, but nothing else, and they are then required to carry on with normal 'morning stables' and prepare their horse to be ridden out for exercise. During this the examiners expect to see the grooms check hay nets, remove feed bowls, check rugs, etc., and muck out. Much attention is paid to methodical, purposeful and efficient working, and the examiners note whether the various tasks are done in reasonable time. Excessive slowness is not acceptable in any yard; conversely, speed that precludes thoroughness is equally unacceptable. The examiners also want to see economical mucking out, and they expect a day bed to be put down correctly. Candidates are instructed to quarter their horses before tacking up, including the spongeing of eyes, noses and docks, which is so often neglected. Special note is taken of whether the feet are picked out *properly*. The method of tacking up is also carefully noted to see whether candidates check the fit and safety of the tack thoroughly before mounting.

Candidates are briefed on what is expected of them in the riding section. They are told that the horse is to be exercised − *not* schooled − on a non-hunting or non-competition day. During this section the examiners look for the groom to demonstrate a controlled, progressive routine of work, and to ride the horse in a bold and workmanlike fashion. In their minds throughout they ask themselves, 'Would I feel confident in allowing this rider to exercise my favourite hunter or point-to-pointer?' After a suitable time, candidates change horses, and it should be noted that the horses provided will vary considerably in type and temperament; special note will be taken of the way the more difficult animals are handled. After working on the flat, candidates are instructed to ride their mounts over a short course of small natural fences. At the end of the riding section they must also demonstrate their ability to ride and lead at the walk and trot, with the led horse on the correct side, and they may be asked questions on the Highway Code.

The remainder of the examination is taken up with searching oral and practical questions on other topics in the syllabus. These may include clipping, poulticing, bandaging, trimming, rugging up, questions on veterinary matters, demonstrations of first aid under emergency conditions, saddlery, the ability to remove broken or twisted shoes — indeed anything that a competent groom should be expected to know. Throughout the examinations the examiners pay a great deal of attention to the candidates' manner with their horses, their general approach to the job, their overall methods and tidiness, and whether they manage to achieve an acceptable balance between efficiency and speed.

Although the examiners tend to judge candidates on the overall impression rather than on rigid marking, they make use of the former dressage marking system and grade each test as 'excellent', 'very good', 'good', 'fairly good', 'satisfactory', 'just adequate', 'weak', 'bad', and 'very bad'. At all times the assessment is based on whether the candidates perform the various exercises in a manner that indicates they will be acceptable as good senior staff who can work without supervision. At no time is the examiners' approach a dogmatic one, and they are prepared to accept variations on orthodox methods, always provided the candidates can show that what they are doing works effectively and is safe.

Candidates for the Grooms' Diploma must, as has been stated, have been in full-time occupation with horses for at least eighteen months prior to the examination. The ABRS has a register of approved riding schools, and students wishing to train for the examination might well consider finding employment with one of these. Indeed, the majority of candidates do come from these approved schools. They then know that the training they are receiving is very much along the lines approved by the ABRS. Some, as for the BHS examinations, may find positions as working pupils. The ABRS, in consultation with the BHS, is at present engaged in reviewing conditions of working pupils; further information on this, and all matters connected with the examinations, may be obtained from the Secretary, The Association of British Riding Schools, 7 Deer Park Road, Sawtry, Huntingdon, Cambs, PE17 5TT.

The Grooms' Diploma offers an excellent qualification for prospective senior employees, and more than adequately caters for those who want to make a career with horses but who do not feel that the various instructors' certificates offered by the BHS or the qualifications of the NPS (National Pony Society) are quite suitable for their particular needs.

In addition to the Grooms' Diploma the ABRS also offers two diplomas for riding school principals and proprietors. It was felt that there are a number of people in such positions who have been running successful riding schools for many years, but who have never, for a variety of reasons, taken any examinations. They perhaps did not, at the time, feel that this was necessary, or they may have begun in business before the demand for qualifications became so fashionable. Now they feel they would like some form of recognition to set, as it were, an official seal on their careers. Now that these two diplomas have been introduced, riding school principals and proprietors, even if they already hold other qualifications may well feel that the holding of these certificates is added proof that they are capable of running an efficient and businesslike establishment.

For the Riding Schools Principals' Diploma candidates must be members of the ABRS, be at least twenty-five years of age, and have been a principal for a minimum of five years. A short resumé of the candidate's experience must be submitted on the entry form for the examination.

Candidates will be required to show a good standard

of horsemastership in the following and related subjects:

Feeding, exercise and work
Stable construction and maintenance
Grassland management
Shoeing and veterinary knowledge
Bitting and saddlery
Suitability of horses

Candidates shall be able to show their ability to manage a commercial riding school successfully in all its facets, for example:

Staff and student management
Organisation of instruction and courses
Keeping of records
Insurance
Simple book-keeping

Candidates will be required to teach and demonstrate, showing a sufficient knowledge of paces, straightness and correct use of manège and jumping, as a basis for active practical horsemanship. (Physical disabilities of the candidates will be taken into consideration, or candidates will be required to provide staff to show the above.) The examination shall take place at the candidate's own place of business.

The syllabus, as can be seen, takes into account the fact that a number of principals, while still able to run excellent establishments, do not, because of injury or other reasons, feel able to ride very much, if at all.

The Riding Masters' Diploma, on the other hand, does require that the candidates demonstrate their own riding ability. For entry to this examination, candidates must be at least thirty years of age, be members of the ABRS, and have been in business as principals or proprietors for a minimum of ten years. A resumé of the candidate's experience must be submitted with the application for the examination.

The candidates will be required to:

1. Demonstrate to the examiners their riding ability, although this may only require a demonstration of basic movements at walk, trot and canter and the examiners will take into consideration any physical or age infirmities — such demonstrations to be performed on a horse of the candidate's own choice.
2. Be conversant with current techniques of teaching.
3. Demonstrate their ability to teach to a standard commensurate with Test 10 ABRS Weekly Riders' Tests.
4. Possess a good knowledge of riding school administration.

The last two subjects shall be adjudged both visually and by oral examination. The examinations will take place at the candidate's own establishment and will take approximately one full working day.

3 Working on Studs

No one involved in the horse world can fail to have noticed the remarkable increase in the number of studs in recent years, and while there is cause for concern about some aspects of this boom, it has meant an ever-increasing demand for highly skilled and well-qualified staff. Stud work has its own very special appeal, with the opportunities it offers for caring for foals, young stock, mares and stallions, and no branch of employment with horses calls for more dedication. The work, particularly at foaling time, is exceptionally demanding, and the delightful picture of a young foal with its dam is often seen through eyes that are red-rimmed with fatigue after a sleepless night spent coping with a difficult foaling. But few who work on studs would deny that the compensations are considerable: the satisfaction felt when a favourite mare produces a really lovely foal, or the stud's young stock make names for themselves in the show ring, or the less spectacular pleasure of watching the mares with the current crop of foals grazing contentedly in the field. The majority of studs are involved in a certain amount of showing, and this too, brings its own rewards.

There is an enormous variety of studs where employment may be sought — native pony, riding pony, Arab, Thoroughbred, hackney, and so on, while some may enjoy the challenge of working with some of the lesser known breeds such as Quarter Horses or Appaloosas that are still endeavouring to gain wider recognition in Britain. Some people who seek employment in studs have ambitions to possess their own one day, and of course the more experience they gain the better.

Stud work is highly specialised and anyone planning a career in this field would be well advised to consider working for the National Pony Society's Stud Assistant's

Certificate and/or Diploma in Pony Mastership and Breeding. These examinations, while designed primarily for people working on pony studs, provide admirable training for any type of stud. Entry for both examinations must be preceded by set periods of work and training at a stud, and candidates must produce a certificate signed by an appropriate person stating that the necessary time has been undertaken and completed satisfactorily. Candidates for the Diploma must be twenty-one years of age, and have had three years experience on a stud, while candidates for the Stud Assistant's Certificate must be seventeen years of age, with one year's experience. It is possible that in the future it may become obligatory for the pre-examination experience to be gained at one of the NPS's approved studs, which are situated throughout Britain: intending candidates should check with the NPS at 7 Cross and Pillory Lane, Alton, Hampshire.

The Diploma syllabus is divided into six sections:

1. Breeding
2. Breaking
3. Pony stable management
4. Show production and presentation
5. Riding
6. Agricultural management of stud land.

Although some candidates, especially those who plan to work overseas, take all six sections, it is more usual to make a choice between the riding and the agricultural management of land sections. The examination is both oral and practical. The full syllabus is as follows:

1. *Breeding.* Covering, foaling, weaning, the handling and management of pony stallions and brood mares, knowledge of reproductive organs and their functions, the ability to recognise a prolapse and other abnormal conditions in mare and foal, knowledge of the methods

of pregnancy testing and reasons and various treatments for infertility. The rearing and handling of young stock both in stable and at grass. Sufficient knowledge to be capable of caring for a mare that has developed complications at foaling time, until a veterinary surgeon can be called.

2. *Breaking.* The theory and practice of breaking a young pony from start up to a standard capable of progressing up to any field of equestrian activity including jumping, lungeing, long reining and mouthing a young horse, progressing to use various bits. Backing, obedience, use and reason for wearing boots and bandages.

3. *Pony stable management.* Knowledge of feeding and quality forage of different kinds, watering, bedding, exercise, grooming, clipping and trimming, thorough knowledge of foot and shoeing, proper care of saddlery. Extensive veterinary knowledge and treatment.

4. *Show production and presentation.* The production and presentation of ponies, including mountain and moorland ponies, and their heights, for showing in hand and under saddle, and their transportation. Candidates must be able to plait mane and tail to show standard, according to horse or pony's conformation.

5. *Riding.* Candidates are required to ride to a high standard of equitation, i.e. they should be active and efficient horsemen able to apply the aids correctly on any type of horse/pony they may be required to ride at the examination. They will ride more than one horse/pony of varying temperaments and stages of schooling. To be able to jump with confidence and ability. Knowledge of elementary dressage movements will be expected of candidates, but no advanced work. Knowledge of fitting and use of tack on any of the horses/ponies being ridden is required.

6. *Agricultural management of stud land.* Fencing, grass management, grazing, eradication of parasites, seeds, watering, land draining, gate fastening, mineral test of soil, spraying, fertilisers, poisonous herbage, and design

and layout of stable yard, including foaling facilities.

Each section of the examination takes about half an hour, with candidates being examined individually by a single examiner, and there will probably be a different examiner for each section. The only exception to the individual examination might be in the riding section, where two candidates may be taken together.

The syllabus gives an excellent idea of the range of knowledge expected, but potential candidates may be interested in the type of question to expect and the type of practical test set. In the breeding section, they will probably be asked to put a foalslip on a foal, and to show the examiner how they would expect a foal to lead by the time it is old enough to be taken into the show ring. They could be required to put a bridle on a stallion, lead him out at walk and trot, and stand him out as if for someone who has come to look at him with a view to sending a mare to him. Searching questions are asked about infertility, the care of mares, foals and stallions, with special emphasis on health and hygiene, bearing in mind the recent problems with metritus. Examination on these topics is likely to be extensive, as the holder of the NPS Diploma is expected to be capable of running a stud in the owner's absence. Candidates may be asked to demonstrate with their arms the correct presentation of a foal from the very start of the waters breaking until the head has appeared, and to explain what to do until the veterinary surgeon arrives if an abnormal birth appears imminent. They may be asked how to nurse an exhausted mare, and, most important of all, when to call the veterinary surgeon in any given situation. Questions are likely to be asked on the foal's bowel movements after birth, about its temperature, and the difference between normal and dangerous scouring. Candidates may also be questioned on when the mare should be presented to the stallion following foaling, and why, for example, a mare would keep 'turning' at three or six weeks.

In the breaking section, candiates are given a wide selection of breaking tack from which to choose. The examiners are aware that of all the subjects in the syllabus, this is the one on which there is probably the widest variation of methods and equipment, and provided candidates have satisfactory reasons for their choice, the examiners are likely to accept them, always taking into account efficiency and safety. When the pony has been tacked up, the candidate is asked to lunge it, and will be wise to ask the examiner to act as an assistant. The examiner looks for control, kindness but firmness, correct use of voice and of whip, as well as the necessary change of rein, paces and halts. Next, the candidate long-reins a pony, with the examiner noting lightness of hand, control, and how near or far the candidate is from the pony's quarters. On returning the pony to the stable, the examiner may ask about bitting, and the stages and methods to be used from the time a pony is first lunged until it is backed, and how an assistant would be used.

The emphasis in the stable management section tends to be on feeding both the performance and the breeding animals and it is important that candidates fully understand the difference. They may be given samples of about twenty foodstuffs and additives and asked to identify and comment on them, giving details of what they are used for, how much should be fed, and their function in either rearing or performance. Samples of hay may be produced, and the candidates are expected to distinguish good from bad, and meadow from seed. Questions on bedding are almost certain, and samples of barley, wheat and oat straw presented for identification and comment. Although more searching questions about the management of ponies at grass are asked in the agricultural management section, the stable management examiner may ask about the safety of fencing, provision of water, etc. Extensive knowledge is required of veterinary conditions and their treatment. Candidates must be able to recognise the various ailments of the leg, such as heat in a tendon, joint or foot, and to recognise the formation of a curb or splint. They must certainly be able to recognise the onset of colic. Knowledge of how to treat a horse that has suffered shock is essential, and while candidates are obviously not expected to have knowledge comparable to that of a veterinary surgeon, they are expected to be able to save their employers expense by *not* calling in professional help unless it is really necessary.

The show production and presentation section is very important, as most studs undertake a certain amount of showing, for publicity purposes if nothing else. Candidates may not only be asked to plait a mane, but to explain why, for instance, they would put in more plaits on some animals than on others. Most seem able to manage the mane, but tail-plaiting is, in general, a weakness. Few seem able to grasp the importance of finishing the plait higher or lower on the dock according to the animal's conformation.

The riding section is more or less fully explained in the syllabus. Those who omit this section and pass the other five will be awarded the NPS Diploma (Non-riding). Candidates are asked to ride three animals of different types and temperaments. The standard is equivalent to the Pony Club 'A' test.

The agricultural management section is examined on the basis that the candidate has acquired a farm of about seventy-five acres and is going to turn it into a stud. There are likely to be questions about what enclosures he would make, with the examiner expecting to hear that he would make smaller paddocks near the house and larger ones further away. Candidates need to be familiar with the size of gateways so that tractors can pass through, the height of fences, and the different materials that can be used with safety, the structure of gates and types of fastenings, and if double fencing is used, how far apart they must be. There will be questions about the use of various fertilisers following a soil analysis, and about the rotation of grazing of horses and other stock. Candidates must be knowledgeable about grassland management, the production of hay crops, and the uses and abuses of sprays. Questions may also be asked about the conversion of farm buildings into boxes, and the ideal layout of a yard.

It is clear from the foregoing that a very thorough and extensive practical and theoretical knowledge is expected from those who hope to gain the NPS Diploma. The majority of the most successful candidates have come up through the Pony Club, and have had a great deal of experience with all types of horses and ponies in a variety of situations. The less successful ones are those who, in spite of rather limited experience, think that because they have reached the minimum qualifying age of twenty-one, they must be ready for the examination.

It must be borne in mind too, that the Diploma holder is almost certainly, in future employment, going to be in a position of considerable responsibility, and is going to be dealing with *people* as well as horses and ponies. The examiners therefore look for a person who gives them a feeling of confidence, and who appears to have the personality and approach necessary for junior staff to work happily and efficiently with and for them. Most, too, are likely to teach others in some form or another — perhaps training staff — and the examiners also take this into account in their overall assessment.

The pass rate for the Diploma examination is approximately fifty per cent, and those who just fail may be awarded the Stud Assistant's Certificate.

The latter certificate can, however, be taken as a separate examination by candidates who have attained the age of seventeen years, and have had a year's experience in a reputable stud.

The syllabus is as follows:
1. *Breeding.* (*a*) every candidate must have had experience of handling a pony stallion, and the procedure of covering.

(*b*) foaling, weaning, the handling and management of brood mares, the rearing and handling of foals and young stock, both in stable and at grass, knowledge of common ailments, and knowledge of reproductive organs and their functions.

2.   *Breaking.* (*a*) Candidates should be be able to assess the stage of training which an animal has reached.

(*b*) Candidates must be capable of exercising a young and/or fit animal competently.

(*c*) Candidates must be able to lunge a pony correctly, including knowledge and use of breaking tack, and recognise various mouthing bits.

3.   *Pony stable management.* Feeding and forage, watering, bedding, exercise, grooming, clipping and trimming, theory of shoeing, care of rugs and saddlery. Elementary veterinary knowledge and treatment and care of horses and ponies at grass.

4.   *Show production and presentation.* The production and presentation of ponies, including mountain and moorland ponies, for showing in hand, and their transportation. Candidates must be able to plait mane and tail neatly, and prepare for travelling.

5.   *Riding.* (*a*) Candidates will be examined in riding and should be active and effective horsemen, able to apply seat, legs and hands effectively, and capable of riding an unknown pony.

(*b*) Part of the ridden examination may be on a partially schooled animal.

(*c*) Every candidate must ride without stirrups if asked.

(*d*) A basic knowledge is needed of how and what a horse can jump at a specific stage of its training.

The examination is along the same lines as the Diploma, but the questions set are less searching, and the exercises more suitable for those who are going to be working under supervision. Non-riders may leave out the relevant section, and if successful in the remainder of the examination will be awarded the Stud Assistant's Certificate (Non-riding). For those who elect to take the riding section, the standard is equivalent to the Pony Club 'B' test.

The stud year may be said to start with the arrival of the first foals, and the exact time of the year depends on the type of stud. Foals on Thoroughbred studs arrive rather earlier than those on, for example, native pony studs, for the very good reason that the official birthday of all Thoroughbreds is 1st January, and the early foal is obviously better developed on the day it officially becomes a yearling — a fact of considerable importance in the racing world for which so many Thoroughbreds are produced.

As the NPS examinations have been the subject of the first section of this chapter, it might be appropriate to take the routine of a native pony stud to give some idea of the work involved. (It should be appreciated that this is an outline of one particular stud, and it should not be assumed that all other studs will be identical.)

About two months before the arrival of the first foals, work begins on getting the resident stallion fit for the covering season, by lungeing, loose schooling, and a bit of jumping. Then comes the anxious and impatient time of waiting for the first foals. When a mare appears to be very near to foaling (and they are usually, and inconveniently, expected to do so overnight!), the staff watch her carefully and check her regularly during the evening. By bedtime it is usually possible to tell if she *is* going to foal that night, and if so, she is checked at, perhaps, three-hourly intervals. The staff get to know their own mares, and can predict the foal's arrival with much greater accuracy than they can for visiting mares. When the mare shows definite signs of the birth starting, the head girl or the owner is called, and they supervise the birth, without interfering with the natural processes unless some problem arises. If a particular mare has had difficulties with previous foalings, the veterinary surgeon is notified that she is due, so that he can be available if required. Provided nothing untoward occurs, and once the mare has cleansed and the foal has begun to suckle, they can usually be left on their own.

Stud policy is to turn the mare and foal out during the day as soon as possible, as it is believed that the mare settles better. An indoor school is used for the purpose, but other studs may turn out into a small paddock, provided the fence is closely boarded so that the foal can see it clearly. For the first few days the staff do not lead the foals, they just push them gently with arms around them, to accustom them to being handled. At the end of about a week they put a foal slip on and begin, in effect, the very first stages in the foals' education.

About nine days after foaling the mare is covered, unless she has foaled early, in which case it is usual to wait until the next time she comes in season. It is then a question of watching the mare to see she does not come into season at any odd times, and of trying her again at three and six weeks.

By this time visiting mares are coming to the resident stallion. Smaller studs do not normally foal visiting mares, chiefly because the mares tend to be fairly local and the short travelling distances involved are not too much for them even though they are in foal. On big Thoroughbred studs, however, to which mares come from all over the country, the staff must be prepared to foal the visiting mares.

The daily stud routine begins in the morning, then all the mares the staff think are likely to be in season are tried. Once they know how many are to be covered, they plan the rest of the day accordingly. Ideally, the stallion covers one mare in the morning, another about midday and a third in the late afternoon or early evening. Mares are usually covered every other day, unless one is known to be difficult, when she will be covered every day. The visiting mares are sent home after the six weeks season, when it is reasonably certain they are in foal.

The covering season ends about the middle of July. By that time, the stud's own mares and foals are probably living out, so they do not receive a great deal of handling, but (and this is where stud and show work overlap) those that are to be shown are being prepared. However, no mare is shown until she is tested safely in foal. Those that are not being shown stay out until weaning time in October.

Before weaning, the staff make sure that the foals living out know about eating hard feeds, hay, etc., and drinking from a bucket; the foals that have been kept in are already more familiar with this. Each mare and foal that has been out is brought in at night for about a week to get the foal accustomed to the stable. Then one evening they are brought in as usual and the mare is taken away out of earshot, leaving the foal in the stable with someone watching it. The tantrums begin as soon as the foal realises that its dam has gone, and the top doors of the stable have to be closed to prevent accidents. Colts are notoriously worse than fillies, but they seem to be cross rather than frightened or worried. Usually, after about a day, the top door can be left open, provided there is someone nearby to keep an eye on the youngster. After a few days, they all settle down, and for those that are going to be turned out again, it is usually possible to do so after about three days to a week. Those being kept in for showing go into the school to play.

By this time, the stud year is drawing to a close, and all that remains is routine maintenance of the mares and youngstock throughout the winter. A busy, exciting, rewarding year, which entails a great deal of effort and the acceptance of a great deal of responsibility by everyone concerned.

4 Racing

The public image of racing with its cheering crowds, beautifully turned-out horses and tight finishes ridden out by top-class jockeys is exciting and glamorous. But behind that image, as with almost all branches of the horse world, the reality is a life of dedicated hard work for everyone employed in the industry, from the best-known jockey down to the most junior stable lad or girl. There is, however, an irresistible appeal about the sport that makes racing the only way of life for thousands of people, not only in Britain, but all over the world.

Many young people who enter racing do so with the ambition to become professional jockeys. It must be made clear from the outset that only a very small proportion of those who become apprentice jockeys ever actually get a ride in public, let alone graduate to the ranks of those who make even a modest living as flat race or National Hunt jockeys. The leading jockeys in Britain, particularly those on the flat, can make a very good living indeed, but it must never be forgotten that these are very few and far between, and the average professional jockey has to work exceedingly hard, travel great distances and have his share of good fortune even to make a reasonable living. It must also be remembered that the *riding* life of most jockeys, especially under National Hunt rules where injuries take appreciable toll, is relatively short compared with other careers. Few flat race jockeys, and even fewer of their National Hunt colleagues can continue riding successfully much over the age of forty — indeed, National Hunt jockeys tend to retire earlier, in their middle to late thirties. So anyone thinking of a career as a jockey should give this point serious consideration. A number of retired jockeys find other positions in the racing industry and make a success of them, but the adjustment that would need to be made by an ex-jockey who is forced to start working again as, for instance, a stable lad, is not easy.

However, for the young boy or girl whose heart is really set on racing, the difficulties to be overcome will no doubt be regarded as a challenge rather than as a deterrent. The best way for the school leaver to enter racing is to become an apprentice jockey, but even before leaving school, steps can be taken towards that goal. Very few trainers these days are prepared to teach their apprentices to ride, and they expect them to have had some previous experience with horses. So it really is essential to learn to ride, and if formal riding lessons are financially out of reach, a number of youngsters find that a local riding school or stable may give them a few lessons in return for helping in the yard at weekends or during the school holidays. If there is a local point-to-point stable, so much the better, as experience gained there would be invaluable.

There is one problem that many youngsters with ambitions to become jockeys are quite unable to overcome, and it is the principal reason why so few apprentices ever become fully-fledged jockeys. That problem concerns weight and size. At the age of sixteen, the potential jockey should ideally be under five feet tall and weigh less than six stone. To gain a place at the Goodwood Apprentices School (of which more later) boys must be under seven stone and girls under eight. Anyone outside these limits stands virtually no chance at all of becoming a flat race jockey, although they may, later on, and by different means to be described, *perhaps* become National Hunt jockeys, where the weights carried by the horses are greater.

Assuming that the aspiring apprentice's physique is acceptable, the next step is to write to the National Trainers' Federation at 42 Portman Square, London, W1H OPA, who circulate the names and particulars of those seeking apprenticeships to all the trainers. Trainers then contact prospective apprentices, an interview is arranged, and if successful the youngster is probably offered a place on a three months' trial basis. Some young people are, of course, able to arrange apprentice-ships through personal contacts.

Work in a racing stable is hard, the hours are very long, and a number of would-be jockeys drop out after only a few weeks. But those who survive the first little while and fit in with the rest of the staff will probably make a satisfactory career in the industry in some capacity.

The first few weeks of the apprentice's career are spent under the supervision of an experienced stable lad or girl, learning the routine of mucking out, carrying and putting down bedding, filling hay nets, checking water buckets and so on. There will almost certainly be no riding at all at this stage. During this time, the apprentice should be able to settle in and become accustomed to living in a hostel with other lads, and as this is probably the first time many youngsters have been away from home for more than a short time, it is, to a large extent a period of adjustment. It is also a time during which the head lad and the trainer assess the approach of the newcomer and if, at the end of a few weeks, they feel he or she is really going to fit into the establishment and be a responsible employee, they will allocate a couple of horses to the apprentice to 'do'. This is quite a landmark in the early part of a racing career, and although these horses are likely to be oldish ones rather than spectacular winners, the young apprentice soon becomes very much involved with them, their well-being, and their success or otherwise in races. In due course, a certain amount of instruction is given in the techniques of exercising race horses, and the apprentice learns how to ride racing style, with much shorter leathers than would be approved in ordinary riding schools.

A typical day in the life of an apprentice begins early, at 6 or 6.15, with morning stables, when the 'first lot' (those horses that are going out to exercise first) are prepared. The stable is mucked out, the horse groomed thoroughly, then saddled and bridled ready for exercise. When considered competent, the apprentice exercises his own horses, riding out to the gallops and following the trainer's instructions. In the early stages of preparing a horse for a race much of the exercise will be just walking, but as the animal gets fitter the pace gets faster, and it begins to work hard at half- and full-speed gallops. After exercising for about an hour and a half, the first lot of horses came back to the stables. They are unsaddled, rubbed down to remove sweat and mud, and their feet picked out; and they are fed. It is the apprentice's job to feed his or her horse (under supervision) and subsequently to note if the animal has not 'cleaned up', reporting this to the head lad immediately. When the first lot have been fed, the staff have their breakfast. Then it's back to the stables to prepare and take out the second lot and, in some stables, even a third lot. After exercise, tack must be cleaned before lunch, after which there is some free time until about 4.30, when the horses are once again thoroughly groomed, with special attention being paid to brushing and trimming manes and tails, spongeing eyes, noses and docks, checking for any signs of leg or foot trouble, and oiling the feet. After the evening feed, the horses are carefully inspected by the trainer and the head lad before being bedded down for the night.

The normal routine does, of course, vary on race days — and the first time 'his' horse races is, needless to say, an exciting one for the apprentice. Normally he goes to the course with his horse, having groomed and prepared him beforehand. On arrival the horse is groomed again, then just before the race he must be walked round for some little time to get rid of any stiffness caused by the journey, and to help settle him down. It is especially at this stage that the lad or girl can play a vital part in the horse's performance. Many animals tend to get nervous and excited when they know they are going to race, and a good lad or girl who can instil confidence is invaluable. As the race time approaches the head lad signals for the horse to be brought into the saddling stalls to be saddled, and then the apprentice takes it into the parade ring to walk quietly round until it is time for the jockey to mount. In a number of races during each season there is a special prize for the lad or girl whose horse is judged to be the best turned out − an added incentive to take even more trouble than usual. Once the jockey is mounted, the lad's responsibility is ended until after the race when he meets it as it comes off the track and − if hopes are fulfilled − leads it back to the winner's enclosure.

Some apprentices are sent by their trainers to the Goodwood Apprentice Training School in Sussex, which is financed by the Horserace Levy Board. There they are taught by former jockey Johnny Gilbert as much about working in racing stables and race riding as can be crammed into a very demanding six weeks. They follow the normal stable routine of early rising and getting their horses ready for exercise, and depending on their standard of riding they may go out and exercise much as they would in an actual working stable. The less experienced and skilful may go in the indoor school for further riding instruction. They are all taught the techniques of race riding, such as changing their whip hands and how to ride a finish. The school has ten retired racehorses, so the apprentices learn very quickly the difference between riding a highly strung Thoroughbred racing machine and the quietish horses or ponies most of them will have encountered at the local riding school. The horses are also used to teach the apprentices stable management, and as not all of them are necessarily quiet in the stable they provide very important experience of how to handle the awkward animals that are sure to be met during the course of a racing career. In the afternoons, the youngsters learn such things as minor ailments, and what to look for in the way of lameness and signs of illness, etc., so they can report them to the head lad immediately.

Girls as well as boys are accepted on the course, and it is encouraging for future 'jockettes' to know that, although some find they just cannot take the arduous and sometimes frightening experiences of dealing with wily old racehorses, others do exceptionally well, and go on to obtain good positions in top stables.

After approximately two years, if an apprentice shows real talent, he or she *may* be given the opportunity to ride in public, perhaps in an apprentice race, or on a horse that is known to go well for a lad or girl. The trainer, in this case, applies to the Jockey Club for a licence for the apprentice to ride in public, and for a few — a very few — the great day comes when they ride their first race. All they have learnt must now be put into practice. But first there is the excitement of donning racing colours for the first time, of sensing the atmosphere and camaraderie of the weighing room, weighing out, and walking into the parade ring to greet the horse's connections and to receive last minute instructions from the trainer. Then comes the moment of being legged up into the plate for the very first time 'for real', and going down to the start, praying, no doubt, that the horse doesn't take off. Down at the start, the apprentice should be fully occupied with settling his horse before the nervy business of loading into the stalls; there are the last few nail-biting moments before the 'off', and the race is under way. Win, place, or lose, few jockeys will forget their very first race. For some it paves the way to a sparkling career, for others it may be the first of the few public rides they enjoy before returning to the anonymity of routine stable work.

Some apprentices do, of course, make a considerable name for themselves while they are still serving their apprenticeships. It is important, however, for even these comparatively successful young jockeys to appreciate that apprenticeship is, in some ways, a rather sheltered world, in which they have the advantages of weight allowances when riding, of their trainer making all the riding arrangements and choosing the right horse for them, and so on. Once the apprenticeship is finished (and these days, most apprentices sign on for a year at a time, renewable by further agreement), and the newly-fledged jockey has to ride in open competition, the going can become very much tougher, and unless the young rider can keep his or her name well in the public eye (and in trainers') reasonably consistently during the first year or so after apprenticeship, the chances of success become depressingly remote. Some young jockeys find that weight problems overtake them, and while a number may switch to National Hunt racing, others find they have to accept that race riding is just not for them.

National Hunt racing does, of course, offer more opportunities for heavier jockeys, and it also offers some chance to a few riders who have not served formal apprenticeships. A number of really good professional National Hunt jockeys begin their careers in the point-to-point field, then, if they have the right contacts, they may be given rides in amateur races under Rules, then in open races as an amateur and finally, they may apply for a professional licence.

But for those young people who at sixteen are already too heavy or tall to ever make a jockey, but who still want to work in racing, there are plenty of opportunities to obtain employment as stable lads or girls. In this, weight is not quite so important, although eight and a half to nine stone is probably about the upper limit for anyone looking for employment in a flat racing yard, and up to ten stone maximum in a National Hunt yard. Although stable hands do not have the excitement of race riding, they do have the enormous satisfaction of looking after the horses, and the thrill and the rewards if 'their' horse wins or is placed. At the time of writing there is a definite shortage of labour in racing stables, and although the wages are not huge (they compare with agricultural workers) there is now a basic minimum, and there are various financial incentives if the horses do well.

After many years of experience, a stable lad or girl may be promoted to the extremely responsible position of head lad of a yard, or travelling head lad, or in a few instances may even become an assistant trainer. It is really not possible to give very much advice to people who think they would like to become trainers. Whilst a stable lad or girl may eventually be promoted to assistant trainer, unless he or she has considerable financial resources, actually setting up independently is probably out of the question.

Young people with the necessary GCE 'O' level qualifications and ambitions to make a good career in the racing or thoroughbred stud industry might consider applying to the West Oxfordshire Technical College for admission to their Stud and Stable Husbandry course. This course is designed for and aimed at those who *do* want to enter those branches of the horse world, and provides admirable practical and theoretical education leading, in most instances, to good positions in the industry. The course is described fully in Chapter 16.

The Veterinary Profession

The first thing to be said to anyone planning to enter the veterinary profession is, 'Give serious consideration to an alternative career to which you can turn if you are unable to obtain a place in a veterinary school.' This is not defeatist, it is absolutely essential, as statistics show that it is more difficult to gain admission to the degree course necessary to qualify as a veterinary surgeon than to any other university course in Britain. According to the booklet issued by the Royal College of Veterinary Surgeons, there are about five applicants for every place available in veterinary colleges in Britain, but individual schools may have as many as 1200 applications for the forty to sixty places offered each year.

For those who nevertheless are absolutely determined to aim at the veterinary profession, preparation for university entrance begins at the GCE 'O' level examination stage at school. Prospective students must, of course, fulfil the matriculation and/or entrance requirements for the six universities in the United Kingdom that offer degrees in veterinary science. In general, this means a minimum of five passes in approved GCE subjects, including two at Advanced level. For those educated in Scotland, passes in five approved subjects in the Scottish Certificate of Education are required, including three Higher Passes. According to the Royal College of Veterinary Surgeons, students with passes in Scottish Highers only (as distinct from 'A' levels) will find their choice of university limited. The actual subject requirements laid down by each of the six universities for entrance or matriculation (Glasgow, Bristol, Cambridge, Edinburgh, Liverpool, and London) vary, and intending students should ascertain individual requirements. In general, however, 'O' level passes in English language, a language other than English, chemistry, physics, biology, possibly some branch of mathematics, and a pass in the use of English is recommended as satisfying the requirements for the majority of universities. In addition to possessing university entrance or matriculation requirements, intending students must also satisfy veterinary degree course requirements. These normally mean a pass at 'A' level in three subjects — usually physics, chemistry and biology; other combinations are sometimes accepted, but again, students should check with the individual universities.

As might be expected with competition for places being so keen, very high academic standards are required, and those offered places are usually expected to gain their three 'A' levels with a combination of A and B grades. There has been some criticism that these very high academic demands exclude the slightly less brilliant student who might, nevertheless, make an extremely good veterinary surgeon. The authorities maintain, however, that on the occasions when they have accepted students with lower qualifications, they have almost invariably found the academic standard of the degree course extremely difficult to achieve.

As prospective university students probably know, application for degree courses must be made through the Universities Central Council on Admissions (UCCA), and the filling in of the application form always arouses doubts and difficulties, not least because of the problems of stating preferences for one university rather than another. Candidates are able to apply to five universities, and are given the option of stating those in order of preference, or of bracketing them together as being of equal perference. The booklet available from the Royal College of Veterinary Surgeons has some helpful comments to make on these problems. It advises those who plan to bracket the five universities of their choice together as being of equal preference to list them in alphabetical order. But it goes on to say that most universities give first consideration to those candidates who have placed them unbracketed at the top of their list of preferences. They will also probably give consideration to those placing them second on the list and, more rarely, to those who place them third. The booklet then goes on to suggest that, bearing in mind that four out of five candidates are *not* going to obtain a place on a veterinary course, serious consideration should be given to using the last two of the five spaces to apply for alternative courses (such as agricultural science, natural sciences, physiology, etc.) where there is less difficulty in obtaining acceptance. The Royal College has been assured by the relevant university veterinary college authorities that such an action will not be interpreted as showing lack of determination or motivation, but rather as indicating common sense. Prospective students intending to apply to Cambridge must make an earlier direct application to one of the University's colleges as well as applying through UCCA, and students who intend to apply to Glasgow as their *only* choice should submit their applications direct to the University.

In spite of the very high academic grades required, many candidates do achieve them, consequently other factors are taken into consideration by the college authorities when making their choice of students. Head teachers' reports, other interests, background, and possibly a personal interview, all play their part. In addition, a recent government report recommended that all candidates for veterinary courses 'should be advised to spend a suitable period with a veterinarian in practice' and indeed the Royal Veterinary College of London University now requires that intending students should visit a veterinary surgeon or any branch of the profession before entering the College. Details of any experience of this type gained by students, or any time they have spent working with animals on farms, kennels or in stables should be included in the 'further information' section on the UCCA form.

Although the veterinary profession has tended to be

male-dominated in the past, the passing of the Sex Discrimination Act has ensured that no discrimination whatsoever is exercised on grounds of sex in considering applications from prospective students.

It should be mentioned that there is a veterinary degree course at the National University of Ireland, University College, Dublin, which is recognised in Great Britain. Further details may be obtained by writing direct to the College.

Having been one of the fortunate few to obtain a university place, the veterinary student embarks on a course that lasts anything from four years and two terms (London) to six years (Cambridge). Those who hope to concentrate on working with horses must appreciate that at undergraduate level no specialisation is possible. A veterinary student in Britain undertakes a comprehensive course dealing with a wide range of animals, and it is not until after qualification that any form of specialisation can be considered.

The actual structure of the degree course varies from college to college, and intending students should apply to each for details. Nevertheless, the subjects covered are much the same, even if the order in which they are studied differs.

In general, the first two years are spent in the study of the basic sciences such as anatomy, physiology and biochemistry, so that students become familiar with the structure and function of the animals with which they will have to deal. Nevertheless, every effort is made to introduce students to the examination, handling and management of animals during these two years, by means of short courses in clinical methods and animal management. The middle years are devoted principally to the study of the nature of disease, by means of lectures, practical classes, demonstrations and tutorials in pharmacology, pathology, microbiology, parasitology, bacteriology, animal health and husbandry. In the last years detailed study is made of clinical medicine and surgery. Students also attend lectures and demonstrations in meat inspection, food hygiene, preventive medicine, veterinary public health and state medicine, and the law as it affects the veterinary profession. Other topics which are introduced at the appropriate stages include histology and embryology, animal behaviour, genetics, statistics, nutrition, clinical pathology and clinical biochemistry.

Students also spend time on the college or university farm, or on farms to which the college has access, to learn the techniques of such things as pregnancy testing, to treat animals, and to see how preventive medicine works in practice. In addition, practical clinical training is given in the college's veterinary hospital where students learn about clinical reception, case recording, diagnostic techniques with the aid of X-rays and laboratory investigations, and medical, surgical and anaesthetic procedures.

All students are required to undertake practical work during the vacations. In the early years a minimum of six weeks must be spent working with farm animals or with live-stock enterprises, while in the senior years, students spend twenty-six weeks in extramural tuition given in veterinary practices, laboratories, investigation centres and abattoirs. Arrangements are made by the veterinary school staff to ensure that the experience thus gained is relevant to the degree course. Professional examinations are normally held at the end of each year, and after passing the final degree examinations, students qualify to become Members of the Royal College of Veterinary Surgeons, and are thus entitled to practice as veterinary surgeons.

Some students, whose examination results warrant it, take advantage of the opportunity offered by all colleges to intercalate a year spent in studying a subject such as anatomy, physiology or biochemistry, to qualify for an honours degree in science, and they then continue their veterinary course as graduate students.

During their undergraduate course, students with a

particular interest in equine veterinary surgery will have plenty of opportunities to decide how they are going to establish themselves in their chosen field. The majority of new graduates go into private practice as assistants, and while in some practices each veterinary surgeon deals with all types of animals, small and large, in others there tends to be some specialisation, with one member concentrating on small animals, another on farm animals, and yet another on horses. There are, of course, practices that deal almost wholly with horses and ponies, taking care of the day-to-day illnesses and injuries at local stables, and attending or being on call for events held at local race course, horse trials, shows, and endurance rides. They may also be called on to perform statutory duties for local authorities concerned with the licensing of riding establishments.

Some graduates prefer to enter the field of equine veterinary research, either at a veterinary college, or an equine research station, while others, after suitable postgraduate training and study, make a career in lecturing or teaching. A number of graduates embark on a varied and interesting career in the Army Veterinary and Remount Services. Most enter on a two-year short service commission with the rank of lieutenant, with promotion after a year's service to captain. Short service officers may apply for a regular commission and remain in the Army until they are fifty-eight. Service veterinary surgeons deal chiefly with the horses in such units as the Household Cavalry and the King's Troop, Royal Horse Artillery, and also with Army dogs, in addition to being concerned with animals owned privately by service men and women. They are also involved in the managerial aspects of animal training units. Service veterinary surgeons are given opportunities for research work, and are encouraged to develop specialist interests.

Veterinary surgery is probably one of the more lucrative careers associated with horses, but it almost always involves long hours, hard physical and mental work, dedication, and, of course, great professional skill. Nevertheless, for those who overcome all the difficulties of gaining a place at veterinary college, and, when qualified can accept the inconveniences of disturbed nights and the necessity to be out in all weathers, veterinary surgery offers an interesting, varied and rewarding career.

Veterinary nursing is a career that appeals to a number of girls who are interested in animals in general and horses in particular. There is a course of training (details may be obtained from the Royal College of Veterinary Surgeons), but this deals almost exclusively with small animals. There is no course of training in veterinary nursing dealing with horses. Nevertheless, the course in veterinary nursing would *perhaps* be useful, as the student would undoubtedly learn the techniques of handling sick animals, and become familiar with veterinary medical and surgical procedures. It would not, however, automatically qualify them to work with horses. Probably the only course of action open to a person really keen to work in this field would be to approach individual veterinary surgeons known to work principally with horses, and enquire if there is any likelihood of obtaining a position in the practice.

6 The Mounted Police

Life as a Mounted Branch officer in any of the police forces in the United Kingdom offers, in effect, a dual career. The mounted officer is able to perform an important service to the community while at the same time pursuing his or her own interest in horses. There are the added advantages of a formally structured and interesting career, with reasonable remuneration, possibilities of promotion, and a pension on retirement. It is thus somewhat surprising that comparatively few recruits enter the police with the clear intention of transferring to the Mounted Branch as soon as possible. Taking the Metropolitan Police as an example, only about five per cent of recruits to the Mounted Branch have had any previous experience with horses.

In the Metropolitan Police, volunteers (whose numbers always exceed the vacancies) must first have completed two years' duty 'on the beat' as foot constables before starting a twenty-two-week equitation and horse management course at Imber Court, the training establishment in Surrey. Apart from an interest in horses and general suitability, recruits (other than those with previous riding experience) must normally be under twenty-five years of age, and weigh not more than eleven stone. There are sound reasons for the weight limitations. A man weighing eleven stone at twenty-five will probably weigh twelve stone at thirty-five; add to this basic weight at least a stone of equipment, and consider too that a police horse's work is mostly on hard roads, and it can be seen that a heavier man might not only appear under-horsed, but would put extra strain on the horse's legs.

On arrival at Imber Court the recruits spend the first few days settling in and absorbing a series of hints about horses that seem to sum up the police attitude to horses and training that produces such excellent results. Such comments as 'the charm to be found in horses is that there is always something new to learn', and 'the real lover of horses should be a student of equine psychology and will find in a horse those qualities so esteemed in man — courage, unselfishness, fidelity', and 'endless patience and progressive training are the only ways of obtaining the best results'.

The twenty-two-week course at Imber Court is divided into five sections, each terminating with an examination, and throughout, theory and practice are correlated by a series of lectures and demonstrations in all branches of equitation and horse management. The basic principles of equitation are very carefully consolidated, and the first weeks of the course are spent learning how to sit correctly and how to control the horse at the walk and trot. A great deal of work is done at the walk and trot before cantering is begun in the fourth or fifth week. In police riding, as in other forms, an independent and balanced seat is essential, and with this end in view a considerable amount of work is done without reins and stirrups.

From about the fourteenth week the emphasis is increasingly on the special skills of riding required by mounted officers. For instance, lateral movements and reining back have a special significance in crowd control; riding with the reins in one hand must be mastered, and particular consideration must be paid to the riding and care of the horse on the road. In addition, police training such as truncheon drill, correct turn-out in full kit, and duties at ceremonial occasions, meetings, and processions are covered, both in theory and practice.

Mounted officers normally patrol singly, and although they are linked to their station by personal radio, they must be ready to deal with emergencies on their own initiative. In preparation for this, trainees do a considerable amount of individual mounted work and road work in company, from about the seventeenth week of their course.

At the end of the twenty-two-week course, which is regarded as preliminary training, the mounted constable is posted to a police station. This is usually one of the larger stables in the Metropolitan area where there are a relatively large number of horses on which the newly posted 'mounted reserve' gains further experience on patrol before being allocated a horse of his own after approximately six months.

Mounted officers work in three shifts. The 'early relief' is from 6 a.m. until 2 p.m., the 'middle relief' from 9 a.m. until 5 p.m., and the 'late relief' from 2 p.m. until 10 p.m. (with a few variations according to circumstances). When members of the early relief come on, their first task is mucking out and grooming their allocated horses and any spare ones. They may possibly quarter the late relief's animals as well. When they have breakfasted, they kit up and patrol the streets from 9 a.m. until noon. If they happen to have more than one allocated horse, they take them out one after another, and are, of course, allowed more time to change tack, groom, and tack up again. The middle relief groom their allocated horses when they come on duty at 9 a.m., set fair the stables, and spend the remainder of the morning doing various 'house-keeping' jobs such as polishing brass-work, hanging up pillar chains, sweeping the yard, etc. They then patrol from noon until 3 p.m. The late relief, coming on at 2 p.m., groom their horses and patrol from 3 p.m. until about 6 p.m. Normally, the police do not like mounted officers to be out on patrol after dark, so on the shorter days they usually come in at about 5 p.m. and see to the remainder of the horses.

Each relief as it comes on takes part in feeding the horses at the stipulated time. Each man, when he has finished his patrol on either the early or middle relief, has to groom his horse again, and clean his tack and boots. The late relief, when they come off patrol, put down the beds and settle the horses for the night, giving them their hay, checking water, rugging up, etc., before going off duty. In stables where there is no night duty (and those are the majority) the station officer in charge of the ordinary police visits the stables at two-hourly intervals during the night to make sure all is well. If there is any problem he phones one of the mounted officers, and thus the horses are cared for throughout the twenty-four hours.

Mounted officers are trained to deal with exactly the same kind of situations as other officers, but their main function is crowd control, at which they excel. They also patrol open spaces such as (in London) Hampstead Heath, in an attempt to prevent attacks on women and children, and similar crimes. The problems presented to a mounted officer if confronted with a crime such as a break-in are exactly the same as for any other policeman except that he also has to decide what to do with his horse. Fortunately, in London at least, the general public is nearly always helpful. If an officer dismounts, people often come forward and offer to help, and it is usually possible to find someone who can safely be asked to hold the animal while the officer deals with the crime. There can be times when this presents difficulties, but mounted officers are trained to use their initiative, and in a real emergency they are, of course, able to contact their station by personal radio.

Although the majority of mounted officers are engaged in patrolling duties, a number are attached to the various training establishments throughout the country as instructors, while others are engaged not only in training new recruits but in breaking and schooling police horses.

7 The Army

The combination of Service life *and* the opportunity to work with horses for at least some of their careers attracts a number of young men. This combination is found in the two principal mounted units of the Army: the Household Cavalry Regiment, and the King's Troop, Royal Horse Artillery, of which the Household Cavalry is by far the larger with a strength of 250 horses and 300 officers and men.

Young men wishing to join the Household Cavalry as mounted dutymen must be between seventeen and twenty-five years of age, weigh at least 130 lb, and be a minimum of 5 feet 8 inches in height. Junior soldiers must enlist between their sixteenth and seventeenth birthdays, weigh at least 125 lb, and be at least 5 feet 8 inches tall. Although there is no formal educational requirement, they must be of reasonable intelligence (as determined by a test) to enable them to absorb and retain information regarding horses and also about modern armoured fighting vehicles, as those making the Household Cavalry their career are likely at some stage to serve with the Armoured and Armoured Reconnaissance Regiments of the Household Cavalry. All entrants should be without a stain on their characters. Although no riding experience is necessary, they must obviously be keen to work with horses, and experience in animal management could be helpful.

After enlistment and completion of his basic military training the young trooper goes to the Household Cavalry Regiment's Hyde Park Barracks in Knightsbridge, London, for the next eight weeks to begin a course of instruction in riding, stable management, and horse care. With up to sixteen other newcomers he joins a Khaki Ride (so called because khaki, as distinct from State uniform is worn) and spends up to an hour a day in the indoor riding school learning the basics of riding from an NCO instructor under the supervision of the Riding Master. Although troop horses, as seen on duty at Horse Guards and in the Sovereign's Escort on State occasions, are used, they are usually older animals that respond to the instructor's voice, and are reasonably quiet. Even so, as the ride almost certainly has a number of troopers who have never sat on a horse before, the early days can be quite exciting. Stable management and horse care is taught by a Corporal of Horse in the regimental stables at the barracks.

At the end of eight weeks, the new troopers are ready to face the first big test of their cavalry careers — a four and a half to five hour ride down to Windsor, escorted by mounted police and motor cycles. At Windsor they do further work in the indoor school, with special attention being paid to their positions in the saddle. They also begin section drill, learning manoeuvres such as turning across the school in pairs and in fours, and dressing, which will be used when taking part in cere-monial duties. There is the added advantage of being able to ride in Windsor Great Park, where they learn to control their horses in the open, and to school over some small natural obstacles. The horses enjoy the stay at Windsor as it gives them a chance to see some open countryside after duties in London.

At the end of the eight weeks at Windsor, the troopers have stable management tests followed by their Khaki Pass Out, for which they must show that they can control their horses at walk, trot and canter, do a circle, and negotiate a jumping lane with a series of cavaletti and a small jump at the end, taking their jackets off as they do so to demonstrate that they have acquired a secure balanced seat without resort to the reins.

After a long weekend's leave, the new entry return to Knightsbridge to begin the final four weeks of initial training, known as the Kit Ride. During this time they learn to ride in almost full State ceremonial uniform

(State kit) of long jack-boots, helmets and cuirasses — although to save wear and tear they have blue patrol jackets under the cuirasses instead of the blue or scarlet tunics. Riding in State kit presents several problems, the most obvious being the necessity to ride with the reins in one hand and a sword in the other. In addition, the long jack-boots require a greater length of stirrup leather and this, together with riding with a sheepskin on the saddle places a premium on good balance rather than grip. A horse tripping can spell disaster to the rider in State kit, as he will have real difficulty in staying in the saddle.

Initially, the Kit Ride takes place for one and a quarter to one and a half hours six days a week in the indoor school, but later on it goes out in Hyde Park to practise troop drills, with turns, troop into line, turning by section, etc., and may take up to about two hours. At the end of the four weeks, the troopers pass out and become Mounted Dutymen B3, ready to undertake Queen's Life Guard and be part of the Sovereign's Escort on State occasions.

The daily and yearly routine of the Household Cavalry Regiment naturally enough revolves around ceremonial duties. The Regiment has a commitment to mount the Queen's Life Guard every day of the year except during the three weeks of their summer camp, when the King's Troop, Royal Horse Artillery takes over. Also, they find the Sovereign's Escort at various State occasions in London such as the Queen's Birthday Parade, State visits, and the State Opening of Parliament. Less routinely, they provide escorts of varying strengths for the Queen or other members of the royal family at special royal occasions outside London.

The daily routine is based largely on the mounting of the Queen's Life Guard at Horse Guards, and, of course, on the general care of the horses. A typical day begins with Reveille at 6 a.m., followed by Reveille Stables at 6.20 a.m., when everyone is down in the stables to feed and muck out. Each man normally looks after the horse that he rides because, apart from the bond that develops between the two, a man is much more likely to take a pride in an animal if he feels it 'belongs' to him. Horses that are not going on guard duty are exercised around the adjoining streets from 7 a.m. until 8 a.m., while the men who are going on guard have their breakfast. Following exercise, tack is cleaned, and anyone who grumbles at *ordinary* tack cleaning might spare a thought for the Household Cavalry − the buckles etc. on the bridles are all brass, and Brasso and leather do not mix terribly well!

After breakfast, the men going on guard duty change into State kit, while the rest turn out the horses ready to go on guard. At 9.45 a.m. they are formed up, and checked by the Regimental Corporal Major at 10 a.m. At 10.05 the Adjutant does his inspection, during which he checks the cleanliness of the horse, the horse's furniture, the man, and his uniform. Marks are given for this, and on these marks depend what the man does while on guard duty − those with the highest marks are allocated the best duties, so there is a definite incentive to be well turned-out.

The Queen's Life Guard leaves Knightsbridge at 10.32, as it takes twenty-eight minutes to walk to Horse Guards, and arrive there just as the clock on Horse Guards Arch begins to strike 11 o'clock. The Guard is changed, and the Old Guard must not leave Horse Guards to return to Knightsbridge before 11.23, otherwise they will pass Buckingham Palace before the Foot Guards are in position to present arms to the Queen's Life Guard. While at Horse Guards, the troopers and horses on sentry duty outside take turns of an hour each.

Meanwhile at the Barracks, the remaining horses are groomed from 11 until about 11.50, when the stables are set fair for lunch. Feeds are prepared and the horses fed at 12.20, while their riders lunch from 12.30 until 2 p.m. Those going on guard duty the next day may be lucky enough to have the afternoon off to clean their kit, while the remainder may either have some time off after lunch until about 3 p.m., or if there is something to be done in the stables they will be there. At 3.30 beds are put down, haynets filled and preparations made for the 4.20 feed. After the evening Guard Mounting Parade at 6.15, the Orderly Officer does his inspection. This takes about thirty minutes, during which the officer checks that the horses have enough bedding, rugs are on correctly, hay nets filled, and that water is available, etc. The duty farrier checks sick or injured horses, and the Night Guard is given its instructions. The day, which had begun at least twelve hours previously, is then considered over.

That is a *typical* day, but when rehearsals for a State occasion are taking place, the hours on duty may well extend to eighteen or twenty. Because of the obvious problems of London traffic, rehearsals must take place very early in the morning, with Reveille at about 3.30 a.m. and the horses leaving the Barracks for Horse Guards at 5.30 a.m.

State occasions do not usually take place throughout the year, they are normally confined to the summer months, but the Household Cavalry is by no means idle, even if it is seen in public less often. Preparations for ceremonial duties may be considered to start in March, when the Commanding Officer's inspection is held. During this, he has a close look at all the Regiment's horses, making sure they are all fit and well turned-out, and generally refreshing his memory in case he should want any for a particular duty or display. In late March and early April formal Troop Drills begin, in which each troop leader takes his troop into Hyde Park and practises various ceremonial manoeuvres. After several practices at troop level, there is a Squadron Drill when the Squadron Leader comes out to see his two or three troops drilling together. Finally, and most spectacularly, there are one or two Regimental Drills when the whole Regiment goes out in the Park, the coaches are brought up from the Royal Mews and the Escort practises keeping the correct distance from them, as is necessary in State drives.

When all these drills are over, the Regiment prepares for a series of inspections by various senior officers, such as the Silver Stick's inspection, and the Major General's inspection. After these, rehearsals begin for the Queen's Birthday Parade in mid-June, and the ceremonial season really starts. On the Monday following the Queen's Birthday Parade there is the Garter Ceremony at Windsor – one of the few occasions in which the Household Cavalry appears dismounted. There is nearly always at least one State visit, and often more than one, for which a Sovereign's Escort must be provided, before the ceremonial season comes to an end with the State Opening of Parliament in November.

Between June and about mid-August fifteen or twenty men from each squadron go on leave, and the opportunity is taken to send some of the horses away to grass. By the end of August everyone is back, and engaged in getting the horses fit for summer camp, held at Stoney Castle near the Guards Depot at Pirbright in Surrey. For this, the entire Regiment moves, lock, stock, and barrel, and it really *is* a camp. The horses are in temporary lines, and the officers and men in tents. Although it is called 'summer' camp, it begins in September and ends in October, which may or may not be ideal camping weather! However, it is one of the few occasions when horses and men get out of London, and can enjoy themselves on cross-country rides, show-jumping, tent-pegging, sword, lance and revolver competitions, and the like. There is also time for inter-troop sports such as volleyball and tug-of-war.

In December and January there are no ceremonial occasions, so the Regiment takes the opportunity to send men on the remainder of their leave. At this time, too, each troop takes it in turn to go away for ten days to winter camp at a convenient venue such as Twesle-down Racecourse. This is enjoyed as much, perhaps even more than summer camp, because each troop is a self-contained unit, and it is up to the troop officer to keep the soldiers occupied with moderately hard work and some entertainment during that time. One of the main objectives of winter camp is to get every member of the troop up to B2 Mounted Dutyman standard, by improving riding standards and concentrating on free forward movement, smooth transitions, jumping, etc. More advanced stable management techniques such as clipping and trimming are also taught to the less experienced troopers. By the time all the Troops have been to winter camp and all the annual leave taken, the twelve months is complete, and it is time for the March horse inspections once again.

It is not all work and no play in the Household Cavalry. Participation in outside competitive events is actively encouraged in the Regiment. Each squadron has an officer in charge of this type of activity, and if three or four men from each squadron want to compete in, for instance, a hunter trial, the Regiment sends them and their horses off in a couple of boxes. The animals they ride are the normal troop horses, but ones that have shown some ability in whatever event they are planning to enter.

The other principal mounted unit in the Army is the King's Troop, Royal Horse Artillery, famed for its skilful and spectacular Musical Drive performed at the Royal Tournament at Earl's Court and at various horse and agricultural shows during the summer.

A young man in civilian life between the ages of seventeen and twenty-five with ambitions to join the King's Troop as a gunner is normally sent along to the unit's barracks in St John's Wood, London, for a few days. During that time, still as a civilian, he will do ordinary stable work — grooming, mucking out, etc. —

and if he can already ride, he may be put on a horse. At the end of the few days, he will have had an opportunity of deciding if the life-style appeals to him, and the Troop also decides if he seems likely to fit in. If both sides are satisfied, and he can pass the Army basic test in reading, writing and arithmetic, and satisfy the intelligence tests, he goes through the normal recruitment process. He is then sent to Woolwich to do his basic Army and gunnery training at the Depot Regiment Royal Artillery before joining the King's Troop at St John's Wood.

Although the majority of recruits have had some previous experience with horses (and this is an advantage) it is assumed that they have not, and all are put in the most basic ride for equitation instruction. When the instructors consider they have reached the required level of competence (the time taken varies) they are passed out as ready for normal mounted duties. There are three levels of Rides within the Troop, and after further experience the soldiers go on to the second one and eventually to the third, by which time they have also reached the standard required to take the civilian BHS Assistant Instructor's Certificate (if they have not already done so). The latter is a prerequisite to going on the Long Equitation Course of approximately six months duration at the Royal Army Veterinary Corps' Equitation Wing at Melton Mowbray in Leicestershire. Not all King's Troop soldiers go on this course, but it must be taken by those who are seeking promotion to Number 1, that is, to be sergeants in charge of a sub-section.

Life in the King's Troop is centred, to a large extent, round the rehearsals and performances of the Musical Drive, and ceremonial duties such as firing Royal Salutes in Hyde Park and Minute Guns at State Funerals such as those of Sir Winston Churchill and Lord Mountbatten. In addition, the King's Troop provides the Queen's Life Guard at Horse Guards when the Household Cavalry is away at summer camp.

Selection for the Musical Drive is on ability, and before the start of the show season in the spring, the teams begin a series of drive practices. These take place initially in the indoor school at St John's Wood, and are done on foot and without horses at first. The soldiers in the teams are joined together by rope as they rehearse all the movements of the Drive until they know them thoroughly. The gun teams with the horses are then brought in and the movements rehearsed again, first at the trot, and finally at the canter and gallop. Anyone who has seen the split-second timing necessary if accidents are not to occur will appreciate the high degree of skill and discipline involved, and the excitement and the satisfaction of being part of such a spectacular exercise. During the show season, the Drive is performed at agricultural and horse shows (including Royal Windsor) culminating in the well-known and popular appearances in the Royal Tournament at Earl's Court.

Although the King's Troop is in the public eye most often during the summer, work naturally goes on throughout the year. After the end of the show season in the autumn, the remounts (young horses that take over from the older ones as they are retired) are selected by the Commanding Officer from a number brought over from Ireland and kept at Melton Mowbray. These have to be broken and backed by members of the King's Troop down at the Royal School of Artillery at Larkhill in Wiltshire. Selection is done not only on suitability of type, but also with due regard to the colours and sizes required for the teams in the Musical Drive. Each team of six consists of bays, browns and blacks, the leaders being larger horses, the centres medium size, and the wheelers the stocky little horses that provide the brakes when they are galloping. When the remounts return from Larkhill in the new year, they have to be broken to draught in preparation for their work in the Drive. Normally, they are not actually used in draught during their first year, but are 'in detachment', that is, they are ridden behind the guns by the soldiers who put the guns into action. Officers' chargers are also broken and schooled, but they, of course, are not broken to draught.

The ordinary daily routine in the King's Troop begins at 6.30 a.m. when the exercise party goes out under the command of an officer. All the fit horses are taken out, each man riding one and leading two. The route, which is varied as much as possible, takes them round the streets of London, and sometimes, when the grass is growing, they go into Regent's Park and allow the horses to graze a little. The duration and pace of exercise varies according to the time of the year, and whether the horses are already fit, or are being worked up to peak fitness. Usually, they are out for between one and a half and two hours.

While the exercise party is out the stables are mucked out by the soldiers left behind. On return from exercise, the horses are 'knocked down' (given a brush over) and then fed. After breakfast, the soldiers groom the two or perhaps three horses in their charge, clean tack and harness, and the limber gunners polish the guns, and so on. The afternoon is spent in different activities depending on the time of the year — perhaps some jumping, or various types of schooling. At afternoon stables, the horses are knocked down again, rugged up, fed and watered, and when they are finally bedded down, that's the end of the working day for most of the soldiers. A few are left on duty to do the late feeds or to go on picket (guard) duty.

Although routine is of necessity quite strict, each horse in the stables is treated as an individual and, within reason, allowances are made for idiosyncrasies. At one time the Troop had two horses who were great friends, so much so that the soldiers turned their two stalls into a kind of loose box so they could be together. Although separate feeds were put in their separate mangers, both ate from the same one at the same time, and then moved on to the other one!

In addition to the duties at St John's Wood, most members of the King's Troop spend some time during the summer at Larkhill on normal gunnery training. But, as in the Household Cavalry, it is not all work and no play. The Troop has a Saddle Club that is affiliated to the BHS Riding Club movement, and officers and men are encouraged to take part in competitive events such as hunter trials, one of the highlights being the Army and Royal Artillery Hunter Trials at Larkhill.

This chapter has dealt, in the main, with young men entering either the Household Cavalry as troopers or the King's Troop, Royal Horse Artillery, as gunners. Young men wishing to become officers in either unit must first have undergone the normal officer training at Sandhurst. Before being accepted into the King's Troop, an officer must first be recommended from other Regiments of Artillery. On joining the King's Troop, he goes on the Long Equitation course at Melton Mowbray before returning to St John's Wood to take up his appointment.

A prospective Household Cavalry officer has to undergo all the normal selection procedure for entry into the Army; a visit to the Regiment, interviews by the commanding officer and the Colonel of the Regiment, the three-day selection board at Westbury and finally the Standard Military and Regular Commissions courses at Sandhurst. Once he has passed all this he is posted to either the Life Guards or the Blues and Royals. He will serve some two to three years with the service in the armoured/armoured reconnaisance regiment before being considered for mounted duty with the Household Cavalry Regiment in Knightsbridge. It is therefore only the regular or extended short service officer who is posted to London for ceremonial duty. On arrival at Knightsbridge, an officer who has never ridden before does exactly the same equitation and stable management training as new troopers. If, however, he can show the Riding Master that he has had extensive experience with horses, the period of equitation training may be reduced accordingly.

Regular officers of either Regiment of Household Cavalry will spend the greater part of their careers with the armoured or armoured reconnaissance regiments on duty in Germany, Northern Ireland, England or elsewhere. Two tours of approximately two years each is the general rule for mounted duty in a full career. King's Troop officers, too, only spend a short period of their military service at St John's Wood and serve for the greater part with other Regiments of Royal Artillery.

8 Farriery

For the school leaver who enjoys working with horses, who possesses the essential skill with his hands, has good co-ordination between hand and eye, and is fit and agile, farriery offers a career with excellent prospects. The craft of farriery has a long and distinguished history, but until quite recently anyone with the necessary skills (and a number without) could practice as a farrier, even though they may not have had any training or qualification. The passing of the 1975 Farriers' Registration Act changed that unsatisfactory situation, and it is now obligatory for any person practising as a farrier or shoeing smith to be registered with the appropriate registration council, and for new entrants to the trade to undergo an approved apprenticeship and pass the examinations for the Diploma of the Worshipful Company of Farriers. (At present, registration is not compulsory in Scotland, but it almost certainly will be in due course.)

The principal scheme for training farriers is the Farriers' Apprenticeship Scheme, which is administered by the Council for Small Industries in Rural Areas (CoSIRA), in consultation with the Worshipful Company of Farriers and the National Master Farriers', Blacksmiths' and Agricultural Engineers' Association.

Potential apprentices should first have established their aptitude for farriery by working with a registered farrier before a formal apprenticeship agreement is made. Applications for apprenticeships under the CoSIRA scheme must be submitted to the Council at 35 Camp Road, Wimbledon Common, London SW19 4UP, on or before 30th March each year for the intake on the following October 1st. A selection committee examines all applications and interviews all applicants.

Having obtained an apprenticeship (at the time of writing there are more applicants than there are apprenticeships available), the employer, apprentice, and parent or guardian will be required to sign a deed of apprenticeship covering four years, the first three months of which are probationary. During the four years the apprentice is paid wages and is entitled to holidays at the National Joint Wages Board rates, details of which may be obtained from the National Farriers', Blacksmiths' and Agricultural Engineers' Association, 674 Leeds Road, Lofthouse Gate, Wakefield, WF3 3HJ. At the end of the apprenticeship the student farrier is required to take the Diploma of the Worshipful Company of Farriers (Dip. WCF) examinations, and on passing must apply for registration under the Farriers Registration Act 1975, before legally being able to practise.

During the four-year apprenticeship the student farriers attend the Herefordshire Technical College on block release for a period of thirty-six weeks, divided (at present) into two sessions of six weeks over three years. The syllabus at the college is divided into eleven sections with a specified time allotted to each, and the master farrier for whom the apprentice is working is expected to give him planned experience, again for a specified time, in all these sections. The sections are:

1. Induction.
2. The use and control of the farrier's hearth.
3. Tools and equipment.
4. Safe handling of horses.
5. Preparation of the horse's foot.
6. Inspection of the horse's foot; remedial treatment.
7. Methods of measurement.
8. Selection of materials. Working temperatures.
9. Shoe making.
10. Fitting and nailing on.
11. Maintaining methods and working conditions.

Within the syllabus the apprentice is taught the characteristics of horses, the methods of handling them, and how to judge the limits of safe handling without the use of drugs or aids. He learns the use, operation and maintenance of the farrier's hearth and the properties of different fuels, and the selection, use, purposes and maintenance of all the farrier's tools. A detailed study of the structure and function of the horse's foot is made, including the physical properties and growth of horn, and the function of the component parts of the foot. He must be able to appreciate its conformation and recognise malformation, thin soles, seedy toe, thrush, sand crack, brushing, over-reach etc., and understand remedial and preventative measures. The recognition and detection of pain and lameness are of obvious and vital importance, and the farrier is expected to act promptly and give first aid if, for example, he is confronted with a horse having a nail penetrating the foot. Equally important, the student farrier learns when his responsibilities end and those of the veterinary surgeon begin — co-operation between farrier and veterinary surgeon when dealing with lameness, injuries, and corrective shoeing is vital.

Also included in the syllabus are methods of measuring the horse's foot, the selection and properties of the materials used in making shoes, and the temperature control of the metals involved. All aspects of making and fitting shoes for all types of horses from ponies to racehorses to heavy horses are studied, both in theory and practice. Instruction in costing and management techniques is regarded as an essential part of training for a career in farriery, since in most, if not all cases, students set up in business on their own in due course.

The foregoing scheme administered by CoSIRA is designed for apprentices who intend to practise farriery *only,* and none of the allied trades. There is another similar scheme, administered by the National Master Farriers', Blacksmiths', and Agricultural Engineers' Association, which trains apprentices who wish to combine farriery with general blacksmithing. Applicants for apprenticeships under this scheme must be between sixteen and nineteen years of age. As in the CoSIRA scheme, a four-year apprenticeship is required, together with attendance at the Herefordshire Technical College for thirteen weeks during the first year, and eight weeks during the remaining three years. In addition to farriery and general smithing, apprentices taking this course are also given practical instruction in gas and arc welding and bench fitting. They take the same Diploma of the Worshipful Company of Farriers examinations as the CoSIRA students, together with trade tests in black-smithing and allied trades.

The courses at the Herefordshire Technical College are full of interest. In addition to well-qualified full-time staff, visiting experts lecture and demonstrate specialist subjects. For example, veterinary surgeons lecture on all the veterinary aspects of farriery, and people from racing stables talk about the special requirements of race horses.

9 Saddlery

'There is one thing that all our students have in common,' remarked a teacher of saddlery at London's Cordwainers' College. 'They're all horse mad. They nearly all have their own horses, or have worked with them in some capacity.' Saddlery, in addition to being a very satisfying occupation in itself, has a number of things to offer that are conspicuously lacking in some other branches of the horse world. Generally speaking, the saddler does not need to work unsociable hours, remuneration is reasonably good, and in contrast to so many occupations involving horses, it is not just an occupation for the young and fit.

The Cordwainers' College offers a year's course in rural saddlery, and although there are no educational qualifications or aptitude tests prior to admission, each prospective student is interviewed, as the college is looking primarily for people who are strongly motivated and want to work as saddlers more than anything else. Applications nearly always exceed vacancies on the course. Normally, applicants must be at least eighteen, but if they are already apprenticed to a saddler, they may be accepted at a younger age.

One of the most interesting features of saddlery is that it appears to attract people of widely differing ages and from very varied backgrounds. They range from boys and girls coming straight from school, to science graduates, retired service officers, and people who have worked with horses in other capacities, such as farriers, grooms, etc. In the last ten to fifteen years the number of women entering saddlery has increased dramatically, and at present there are often more women than men on the Cordwainers' course.

No matter what their background, all students start the course from the very beginning, and it is assumed that they know nothing about saddlery. They learn about the tools, how to use them safely, how to look after them and how to sharpen them. Next, they are taught stitching — single and double hand stitching, the double hand being with a needle in each end of the thread and crossing all the time. Having learnt the basic skills, the students begin on a syllabus that becomes progressively more advanced. They start by making small items such as rein stops and Irish martingales, and move on to standing and running martingales, girths (it may interest readers to know that there are about fourteen different kinds!), head collars and drop nosebands. Next, they learn to make snaffle bridles, breaking tack (including cavessons and rollers) and double bridles. During the course of the year every student makes a spring-tree all-purpose saddle.

Some students are naturally quicker than others, and when they have finished a particular task, they are encouraged to bring in projects of their own, such as saddlery repairs. A little harness making is taught, and anyone who can find the time to do more of this ever-expanding aspect of the saddlery business is encouraged to do so. Boot repairing is also an increasing part of the average saddler's business and this, too, is taught. Although everything made on the course is hand-stitched, students are also taught machining on the wide range of machines available at the college. There are some things that cannot be done by hand, such as rug repairs, and experience is gained in this.

About three-quarters of the course is practical, as might be expected, but the students acquire a really comprehensive education in all facets of the saddlery trade. They attend lectures on costing, book-keeping, materials science, and the manufacture of leather. The college syllabus also includes liberal studies, as a break from professional training. The students visit art galleries and museums in London, and where possible are taken on a remarkably extensive range of visits to see things connected with their subject. They visit tanneries, go to the Royal Mews to see the magnificent harness and tack there, and visit Imber Court to see the police saddlery workshop. In addition, they go to Stoneleigh for a one-day course, during which there is usually a demonstration or talk by an expert in a particular aspect of riding, with emphasis on the tack used. The students also go to Walsall, the centre of the saddlery manufacturing trade, where they visit three factories. They go to Reading Horse Sales where a large amount of tack and harness is sold, and they usually manage a trip to one of the big shows at Wembley to see the trade stands there and note the standard of the work and the current prices. Visits are also paid to an Arab stud, to the Shire Horse Centre at Maidenhead, and to the Equine Research Station at Newmarket.

The students' work is continually assessed by five different people, and at the end of the course they take the City and Guilds of London examination in rural saddlery, and an examination set by the Worshipful Company of Loriners on bits and bitting. They also take a college examination.

Having passed all the examinations, those who are already apprenticed return to their place of employment, while others obtain positions (often with the assistance of the college) with master saddlers up and down the country. A few go into business on their own, but the college does not recommend this, as they feel more experience is required first.

Not all potential saddlers apply to or are accepted by the Cordwainers' College; some endeavour to obtain apprenticeships with master saddlers in various parts of the country. The Society of Master Saddlers points out that openings are few and far between, and unless the prospective saddler is fortunate in finding a master in his or her own district, the best plan is to write to the Society at 9 St Thomas Street, London SE1, for a copy of the current Year Book, which lists over 250 master saddlers who may be approached. If successful, applicants embark on a four-year apprenticeship with indentures registered with the Society, and at the end of the four years the apprentice receives a certificate signed by the Worshipful Company of Saddlers.

Some masters may send their apprentices to the Cord-wainers' College, while others may take advantage of the scheme run by the Council for Small Industries in Rural Areas (CoSIRA). Under this government-backed scheme called the New Entrant Training Scheme (NETS), the apprentice attends the CoSIRA workshop for a total of ten weeks spread over two years, and is taught the skills of bridle and saddle making and repairing. If the apprentice comes from a workshop which does harness work, this can be taught as well. In addition to the ten weeks the apprentice spends at the workshop, the CoSIRA technical staff pay ten one-day instructional visits to the student in his own place of employment. At the end of the two years, CoSIRA awards each apprentice a certificate, and there is a prize for the most satisfactory student.

The principal aim of CoSIRA is to train people already in various rural crafts, and as well as the NETS scheme, they run short courses for saddlery employees in various aspects of the craft. Many people think that a saddler is automatically able to deal with all kinds of harness making and repairing, but this is by no means necessarily the case. Harness making is a separate (although allied) craft, and CoSIRA provides a certain amount of tuition in this on their short courses. Collar making is yet another separate craft, and there are very few collar makers around today. CoSIRA do not teach this craft, but if a student on one of their courses brings in an old collar, the staff will be able to show him (or her) how to refurbish it.

10 Showing Stables

Life in a showing stable can be a fascinating mixture of long hours preparing and schooling, anticipation and excitement as the shows approach, intense concentration during the classes, and either the elation of success or the disappointment and at times the frustration of not doing as well as expected. For many people the mixture is irresistible, win or lose.

There are almost as many types of showing stables as there are types of horses, and the positions in them range from the most junior groom to the top-class professional show rider or handler with his or her own livery yard from which clients' horses are produced. Positions in show stables are advertised in the equestrian press, and although it is quite possible to obtain one without having any qualifications, the person who seriously intends to make a career would be well advised to undergo some form of professional training.

As anyone who goes to shows will appreciate, there is a considerable difference between producing animals for in-hand classes and producing them to be ridden, but each, at its best, requires great skill, and is an art that can only be acquired over years of practice. Initially, the junior show stable employee is more likely to be concerned with normal stable routine than with the specialised work of producing the horses for the ring. However, preparations for a new show season begin well in advance, and in a stable from which young stock are shown, work on yearlings probably goes on throughout the winter, and the young groom may be asked to assist in this. The yearlings must be taught to stand correctly, to lead easily, and to walk up and trot back so as to show off their best points. Teaching a yearling to stand still can be quite a challenge, and the senior staff member or owner is likely to need an assistant. Usually, one person leads the animal in to a halt, and the other assists by gently pushing from behind or 'rearranging' a leg. This helps to ensure that the animal stands correctly with its head well forward so as to show its front to the best advantage.

Leading a horse or pony *properly* in the show ring is something a surprising number of even very experienced people never learn. Lucky is the show stable employee who is taught that clutching the leading rein about six inches from the horse's head and running along either right beside its head or even just in front of it is a sure way to make it turn its head to one side and so impede free forward movement.

While the yearlings are receiving their ring education they must also be exercised, possibly by loose schooling or by being taken for walks so they become accustomed to a variety of sights and sounds. The two- and three-year-olds in the stable have their memories of ring behaviour refreshed, and they too must be exercised, probably on the lunge. Feeding during the build up to the show season is important, and the youngsters have their food increased according to the amount of work they do.

There are, as always, a number of problems that must be overcome, and the production of colts, whose shows are often early in the season, is often difficult because of getting their summer coats through. Two- and three-year-olds can be, and frequently are, clipped. The same difficulties arise (and not only with colts) at the other end of the season, when winter coats may start to come through too early.

Producing animals for ridden classes is a different art again, and although in this too, the newcomer is more likely to be concerned with their routine care than in producing them, he or she can undoubtedly learn a great deal for the future by watching senior staff or owners schooling for the ring.

All the work of schooling, grooming, and conditioning is put to the test on show days, and the immediate preparations usually start the day before a show. All the tack is cleaned, checked and packed into the lorry or trailer, together with rugs, grooming kit, plaiting kit, food, hay, and water. Some stables wash the horses or ponies the day before, others wash only manes and tails. The actual day begins bright and early, with feeding, grooming etc. and extra time being allowed for plaiting if the animal is in an early class. The horses and ponies are then bandaged and dressed for travelling, before loading and setting off in good time.

On arrival, those due in the ring first must be unboxed, and the in-hand ones walked around for varying times to help them settle and become accustomed to the surroundings. The ridden animals must be worked in. There is an art in deciding just how much work should be done before a class to ensure that the animals are settled but still looking bright and interested. Real babies pose special problems, as they can be full of beans and sparkling one second, and almost 'dead' the next. A number of show stables work their horses for the appropriate time, and then put them back in the box while the final bits of grooming are done.

Who actually does the showing, be it in-hand or ridden, obviously varies from stable to stable, but most handlers or riders need some assistance to be available during the class. In ridden classes a groom has to be at hand to go into the ring when the horses are stripped and give them a quick brush over to remove any unsightly saddle marks. With in-hand classes this is obviously not necessary, but on very hot days a groom may, while the judge is at the other end of the line, put a sheet on the animal just to keep its coat lying down and prevent it from appearing starey.

Staying overnight on show grounds can present its own problems. Apart from having to pack more equipment, including some form of barricade to put across the top of the stable door if an animal is inclined to become excitable, many stables take a supply of water from home in case the show ground water is rejected by the horses. This is especially important in the case of brood mares with foals. In most instances, horses and ponies tend to be quieter and more subdued away from home, and this sometimes manifests itself in a disinclination to feed properly. Many stables take with them a good supply of titbits such as carrots and apples in order to tempt the reluctant feeder, and a number give smaller, more frequent feeds than when at home.

After the show the animals must be prepared for the journey home, and on arrival, no matter what the hour, the lorry must be unloaded, the horses bedded down and, in most instances, the tack cleaned. This can mean an exceptionally long, tiring day, but if the horses have won, it all seems worth it. If they have not met with success -- then there's always next time!

11 Show Jumping

Any young person attracted by the 'glamour' of working in show-jumping stables might ponder on the tribute paid to grooms by a well-known international rider. 'The public haven't a clue how hard the grooms work, often in acute discomfort, and for unbelievably long hours. They're absolutely marvellous.' Certainly some of the show grounds on the national circuit leave a great deal to be desired from the groom's point of view, with stables inconveniently distant from the show rings, and surroundings that become a sea of mud in bad weather, with the accompanying difficulties of wet, dirty horses and tack. Travelling between shows can mean long, tedious hours on the road, sometimes overnight, and the not unknown joy of arriving at a show ground in the small hours and leading the horses to their allocated stables only to find someone else's animals already bedded down there in error.

But of course it's not all tedium and frustration. Life in a show-jumping stable can be, and often is, exciting, interesting and rewarding, and if the groom works for an international rider, there is the possibility of travelling abroad. There is also the attraction of the undoubted camaraderie that exists among grooms who 'travel the circuit', who come to know each other well, and help each other in times of difficulties.

Jobs in show-jumping stables vary according to the level at which the groom's employer competes. At one end of the scale is the 'hobby' show jumper who competes at a number of local shows and perhaps occasionally at the nearest county show; at the other is the top-class national or international rider who travels extensively both in Britain and abroad, returning home from time to time to give the horses a rest and to spend some time bringing on novices. The young groom would be well advised to work in the former type of stable for a while to gain experience before moving on to work for a rider competing at a higher level. It is, in any event, unlikely that a busy national rider would have time to take on and train a comparatively inexperienced groom.

As the majority of grooms who plan to go into show-jumping stables probably *do* have the ambition to work for a leading rider eventually, a brief outline of the routine may be of interest. Indeed 'routine' is probably a misleading word, because apart from the fact that show jumpers, like any other horses, have to be mucked out, fed, watered, groomed, exercised and bedded down, there is little that is routine about their competitive lives, with their constantly changing show grounds and unfamiliar stables. The groom's main tasks are to do all in their power to keep their charges fit, happy and relaxed throughout a packed season, and have them turned out in tiptop condition week after busy week.

In these days of both summer *and* winter show-jumping, the groom for a top rider is likely to be fully employed on the show circuit almost all the year round, although not always travelling the same horses. However, the summer is undoubtedly the busiest time.

Show jumpers almost certainly spend more time travelling and being stabled away from home than any other competitive horses, and the preparations for a tour consisting of, for instance, three two- or three-day shows in about a fortnight are obviously quite extensive. In addition to packing the usual tack, medicine box, grooming kit, bandages, boots, etc. (with spares), a selection of rugs must be taken to suit the variety of weather that could be encountered. Enough food must be loaded into the lorry to last throughout, as it is rarely possible (or advisable) to obtain any en route. This applies particularly when travelling in Europe, as the foodstuffs there are different from the homegrown variety, and can upset the horses all too easily.

Special measures must be taken when travelling the

horses over the very long distances sometimes encountered. Some horses are inclined to go off their feed a little
during a long journey, and under these conditions the
rule is a familiar one, 'little and often'. It is common
practice for the groom to make up a number of short
feeds before travelling, and just tip them into the travelling manger from time to time to keep the animal
occupied. On a really long journey stops must be made
every so often to give the horses a rest, and during these,
bandages should be removed and the legs rubbed by hand
before replacing the bandages. These short stops apart,
most riders prefer to get the journey over as quickly as
possible, even if it means driving through the night. On
arrival at the show ground, a quick brush down and
possibly a short walk round to ease travel stiffness is the
usual routine before settling the animal into the stable
and leaving it in peace. On show grounds, most grooms
sleep in tack rooms, in the horse box or in caravans.

On competition days, the groom must have the horse
ready in plenty of time for the rider to warm it up before
going into the ring. As most stables or horse-box parks
are some distance from the ring, the groom needs to take
rugs, sheets, grooming kit etc. to the ringside, and, where
necessary, studs and a stud spanner.

When jumping is over for the day, the horse has to be
groomed, fed, watered etc. in the usual way and settled
for the night. At the big indoor shows, such as those at
Wembley for instance, with jumping going on late into
the night, it takes little imagination to realise that most
grooms will be fortunate if they have finished work
before midnight, and it is often much later.

At the end of a show, most people like to be away
from the ground and en route to the next as quickly as
possible. A number of owners and riders stop somewhere
along the way and give their horses a change of scenery
with a hack round a field or along a beach before arriving
at the next venue, where the busy round starts again.

Travelling to Europe is usually by ferry and train or box, or, less frequently because of the expense, by plane. Preparations for travelling are much the same, except that an enormous amount of documentation must be carried, and the actual journeys can be traumatic. Delays at border crossings are commonplace, and the frustration of arriving at a crossing just minutes after it has closed for the night is aggravated by the necessity of trying to find stabling in a foreign country, with the usual language barriers. However, there are compensations in the form of, in some countries, beautiful show grounds, luxurious facilities and a chance to meet riders and grooms from other teams and become part of the international show-jumping 'circus'.

Although only comparatively few grooms have the opportunity of working for the top riders, there are plenty of vacancies with less well-known riders, and finding a position should not be too difficult.

Some young people, however, have ambitions to make a career as show-jumping riders, and here the picture is very different. It is only fair to point out that there are very, very few people who make a living out of show jumping as such, and with the overhead expenses as they are, the chances of making a living from prize money or by riding full-time for a big owner are very small indeed. There are a number of people who make their living from horses and their principal competitive activity is show jumping, but on the whole, they rely on buying, schooling on, and selling for the larger part of their income, or have some other form of income to back them up. While there are always exceptions, in general it must be said that, at the present time at least, show jumping as a *full-time* money-making career offers few opportunities.

12 Eventing

The seemingly large sums offered as prize money for major show-jumping classes are generally lacking in horse trials, and few people would consider event riding as a means of earning a living. However, as in show-jumping, there are very attractive positions available for grooms in eventing stables, with plenty of excitment and the added interest of being involved with three phases of competition riding: dressage, cross-country, and show-jumping.

There is less travelling to be done, simply because event horses cannot compete as often as show jumpers, and the opportunities for travel abroad are probably less, although by no means non-existent. Nevertheless, most eventing grooms would not change places with anyone.

To give some idea of what is involved, let us consider briefly the work of a groom looking after an event horse at a big three-day event. The event probably has two days of dressage, so the horse must arrive at least the day before the first of these for the initial veterinary check. For this the horse must be groomed, and walked around to eliminate any travel stiffness. After the vetting, the rider may work the horse for a time, or take it for a short hack to assist in settling it.

If the horse's dressage is the following day, an early start may be necessary, as the rider certainly needs to give the animal some work. For this the horse must be groomed, tacked up and appropriately bandaged. Before leaving for the test itself, the horse must be groomed again, plaited, tacked up and studded (if necessary), and the groom must follow up to the collecting ring with equipment such as rugs, head collar, grooming kit, etc. to give a last minute tidy up before the horse goes into the arena, and to take care of it when it comes out again.

Often, on the first evening of a big event there is a

party for riders, grooms and officials, and this is one of the few occasions when the grooms will have the opportunity of relaxing, and meeting and renewing acquaintances with other grooms and competitors.

Cross-country day is one of tension, and the groom can contribute significantly to the peace of mind of both horse and rider by quiet efficiency, thus allowing both to give their full attention to the tests ahead. After the early feed, and assuming that the horse is starting Phase A (roads and tracks) about mid-morning, he must be groomed, bandaged, booted, and tacked-up ready for the rider to be at the weigh-in at the stated time, complete with saddle and, if necessary, with weight cloth. The groom collects all the equipment required, including spare tack, rugs, sheets, buckets, sponges and something to treat the odd cuts and bruises, and takes them up to the course. When the rider has weighed in, the groom finishes tacking up the horse, and checks that everything is in order before the competitor sets off on the first part of the roads and tracks followed by the steeplechase. Between the end of the second roads and tracks and the start of the cross-country there is a period of about ten minutes during which the horse is usually unsaddled, sponged down, walked around to cool off a little, and if necessary, has his studs changed. He may possibly be given a mouthful of water, or have his mouth rinsed out, before starting on the biggest test of all, the cross-country.

At major events, it is often possible for the grooms to watch the cross-country on closed-circuit television, and at most of them a commentary records the progress of competitors round the course. Grooms naturally become deeply involved in the well-being of their charges, and it is a toss-up as to whether rider or groom is under the greater strain during the cross-country round. But assuming that the horse completes, the rider must weigh in, while the horse is walked round briefly before a quick sponge down, and is then returned to the stables for more thorough attention. A quick drink, treatment of any minor injuries, and possibly another walk round is given before grooming and bandaging and, depending on the time of the day, a feed.

Sometimes, however, things do not go smoothly. If the horse has knocked himself and sustained some injury on the cross-country, it is not unknown for groom, rider and a veterinary surgeon to be up most of the night trying to get the animal sound for the veterinary test which must be passed the next morning. The night after the cross-country can be a very difficult time indeed, and a time when the rider may need a great deal of calm help and support from the groom.

If no disasters have occurred, the horse must be prepared next morning for the veterinary inspection prior to the afternoon's show jumping. A good walk round to remove any overnight stiffness and/or filling of the legs is essential before the animal is walked and trotted up (sometimes by the groom, often by the rider) in front of the inspecting panel. This too, can be a nerve-racking time, particularly if the horse's connections are aware that it is likely to be 'touch and go'.

Having successfully passed the veterinary inspection, the rider will certainly want to work the horse in readiness for the jumping. As for the dressage phase, grooming kit, rugs, etc. must be taken up to the collecting ring, and then all the groom can do is wait, as horse and rider loosen up over a few practice fences before what could be a winning round. Whatever the result, the groom's task is likely to be the same — back to the stable with the horse, with preparations for the homeward journey to be made at the end of a very concentrated three or four days, in which a really *good* groom can do so much more for horse and rider than just the routine duties. A horse that is calm and relaxed performs to the optimum of its ability, and a rider that has confidence in his or her groom is able virtually to forget all the details of horse care, and concentrate on the essential business of competing in a very tough, demanding sport.

Polo Stables

Every year, about the beginning of February, advertisements begin to appear in the horse press for polo pony grooms for the coming season. The essentially seasonal nature of this type of work has its disadvantages, but a number of girls who thoroughly enjoy working with polo ponies do so for the summer, and then find positions in hunt stables or hunter livery yards for the winter. Thus they are rarely, if ever, out of work, and many enjoy the variety of occupation.

Apart from normal stable duties, working with polo ponies involves exercising and working them, and looking after them before, during and after matches. A certain amount of adjustment may be necessary when riding polo ponies for the first time, and those who have not ridden them before must accustom themselves to a different style of riding. A little thought, or even a short time spent watching polo, will confirm that the ponies are ridden chiefly at the canter and gallop and, occasionally, at the walk. (The trot of a good polo pony is said to be most uncomfortable!) Neck reining is the normal method of steering, and leg aids are seldom used. Good ponies respond very quickly indeed to the rider's shift of weight, and anyone without a very secure seat can find themselves sitting on the ground in no time at all.

At exercise, the ponies do little if any road work as they are studded for playing and the hard roads cause such trouble with stud holes. Unless they have become bored or stale, taking them out for a hack is comparatively unusual. On non-match and non-practice days, the grooms probably exercise them for about an hour, and this can include practising galloping flat out and pulling up quickly, and accelerating from a walk into full gallop. At other times, a single groom may exercise up to about five ponies at a time riding one and leading the others cantering in circles. The ponies are remarkably amenable in this respect, having been accustomed to being tied up together during matches and practices. On occasions, grooms may play a part in the basic schooling of young ponies, but in general, players prefer to do this themselves, so that the ponies become used to their way of riding.

At the height of the season, grooms can expect to be involved with perhaps two practice evenings and one or two match days each week. On practice days, the ponies taking part will probably not be exercised, but the others must be taken out as usual. Practice days are long, but match days are even longer. Routine stable duties and exercising non-playing ponies must be done, and tack, gear and playing ponies prepared and possibly boxed to reach the ground by 2 p.m.

During a match, one player plays two or three ponies, and at the end of each seven-minute chukka the groom must have the second pony ready, take it to the player, lead the used pony away to be stripped of its tack, washed down, its bandages checked, and tacked up again, ready to be played again after another seven minutes. At the end of the match, most grooms like to strip their ponies and wash them down at the ground so there is less strapping to do on returning to the stables. Evening practices or matches make a very long day indeed, and if travelling is involved, the grooms and ponies may not get back to the stables until ten o'clock or later.

But in spite of the disadvantages many girls enjoy the job. Polo is a fast-moving and exciting game to watch, and the grooms naturally become very involved in the fortunes of 'their' ponies and the teams of which they are such a vital part. Working with a team of other girls can be fun, and the social life is often very enjoyable.

Trekking and Riding Holiday Centres

Pony trekking and holidays with horses have, over recent years, become a considerable industry, and provide very enjoyable employment for the right kind of person — the person who loves horses, enjoys meeting and dealing with people, and has a cheerful, sympathetic outlook. The person contemplating working in this sphere must appreciate that his attitude can make or break a holiday-maker's enjoyment, and for this, as well as for other reasons, working in a holiday centre is a very responsible position, to which not everyone is suited.

To suggest employment in a trekking stable or holidays with horses centre as a career may not appear wholly realistic, as by its very nature it tends to be a seasonal activity. But some centres *do* employ staff throughout the year, to look after the visitors in the summer, and take care of the horses and ponies in the winter. An increasing number of centres, particularly those near the more populated areas, combine seasonal riding holidays with more formal instruction for local residents throughout the year, and are thus able to offer all-the-year-round employment.

For those who are able to set up in business on their own account, running a trekking centre is a very pleasant (although extremely demanding) way of life, not least because of the satisfaction to be gained from providing people with holidays that they enjoy, and perhaps being the means by which they develop a lasting interest in horses and ponies.

Anyone planning to be involved in the trekking business either as an owner of a centre or as a trek leader or escort would be well advised to get in touch with one of the three national associations that have been formed with the aim of raising standards in the industry, and to operate training and grading schemes for trek leaders, and operators. The most recently formed is the English Riding Holiday and Trekking Association, c/o Approvals Office, The British Horse Society, British Equestrian Centre, Kenilworth, Warwickshire, CV8 2LR. In Wales there is the Pony Trekking and Riding Society of Wales, Tudor Cottage, Llwyndafydd, Llandysul, Dyfed, SA44 6LD; in Scotland, the relevant authority is the Scottish Trekking and Riding Association, Tomnacairn Farm, Trochry, Dunkeld, Perthshire.

The Welsh and Scottish societies hold courses for trek leaders and instructors. Those run by the Welsh Society are held at an establishment approved by the Society, and normally last from Sunday afternoon to the following Friday. The syllabus, taught by resident and visiting lecturers, is eminently practical and covers all aspects of trekking and riding holidays. Candidates are assessed throughout, and topics include basic instruction with emphasis on catching the pony ready for the trek, tying up indoors and outdoors, grooming, saddling, bridling, elementary equitation, the lunch break with procedure towards guests, and the return ride. In the section on trek leading, attention is given to the all-important allocation of ponies to guests, and the guests' welfare, accommodation and entertainment. A full-day ride is undertaken incorporating these points, and at least one of the Society's examiners accompanies the ride to assess the candidates' competence.

Pony type and suitability are discussed, with the emphasis on British breeds and types and their suitability for trekking and trail riding. Horsemastership and veterinary topics are also covered, as are farriery and saddlery with special reference to the safety and comfort of both pony and rider. Candidates are expected to be familiar with the Highway Code as it affects horses and riders, and with the requirements of the Riding Establishments Acts of 1964/70. It is not possible to include a *full* course of first aid in the five days, but a qualified lecturer covers the basic and most essential points necessary to deal with any injury sustained by a trekker. Country lore and rights of way are also studied. During the course, a written paper of an hour's duration is set to assist the examiners in their final assessment.

Grades may be awarded as follows:

Grade I. Competent to take full charge of a trekking centre. To obtain this grade, candidates must be eighteen years of age or over and must have worked a minimum of one season at an approved trekking centre or already hold the Society's Grade II certificate.

Grade II. Competent to take charge of a trekking centre under the supervision of the operator (minimum age sixteen years).

Grade III. Competent to take charge of a trek (minimum age sixteen years).

Grade IV. Competent rider, able to assist on a trek.

Provision is also made for students to take the BHS Road Safety Test if they so wish, but this is not included in the candidates' final assessment.

The courses are aimed at both employers and employees of centres, with the employers doing an additional section on the more administrative side of the business, such as records and methods of booking. On the Thursday evening of each course, the Society invites operators from other trekking centres to attend to meet the students, and possibly offer them employment for the coming season.

The Scottish Trekking and Riding Association runs two courses for Instructors each year, one in March and one in October; the one in March includes a week's training at a Pony Trekking Centre. The syllabus is as follows:

General. Candidates will be expected to have studied the Scottish Sports Council *Notes for the Guidance of Pony*

Trekking Leaders and the *Guide to Pony Trekking Operators,* also the Highway Code so far as it refers to horses and horsemen (see RoSPA's publication *Riding and Roadsense*).

General knowledge. A knowledge of the countryside and country manners (see *Country Code*).

First aid. A working knowledge of first aid. (The British Red Cross Society's *Junior Manual* is a good guide.)

Riding ability. Candidates should be able to mount and dismount correctly, walk, trot and canter, and be able to lead another pony from the saddle. They should also display assurance and dexterity in the saddle.

Horsemanship. Points of the horse, conformation, and a general knowledge of British breeds and types and their suitability for trekking and trail rides. (*The Observer Book of Horses and Ponies* is a good guide.) Feeds, feeding practice and a knowledge of grazing. Watering. Health: recognising ill health, lameness, saddle and girth injuries. Housing and shelter. Grooming. Shoeing and care of the feet. Tying up, indoors and outdoors. Tack: knowledge of saddlery, care of saddlery, fitting of saddlery, safety and comfort of pony and rider. Elementary veterinary knowledge and first aid.

Trek organisation and management. Organisation of a centre: ponies, staff and facilities, organisation of a trek, responsibility to riders and operators, routes, access, countryside behaviour, trekkers' welfare, accommodation, and entertainment.

Candidates may be awarded the following grades:

Grade I. Competent to take complete charge of a pony trekking centre. (Before being awarded Grade I, instructors must be twenty-one years of age or over and have worked one season at a pony trekking centre, or have equivalent experience at a riding establishment. In this connection a testimonial from an employer will be required.)

Grade II. Competent to take charge of a pony trekking centre under the supervision of an operator.
Grade III. Competent rider, able to take charge of a trek.

The Association operates an employment register to help centres find staff, and instructors to find employment.

The English Riding Holiday and Trekking Association is, as has been mentioned, the most recently formed of the three societies, and it too, hopes to hold Ride Escorts' and Trek Leaders' courses in the future.

Work at a trekking or riding holiday centre is demanding, but there are the compensations of, in most cases, riding through and getting to know some of the most lovely areas of Britain, and of having the satisfaction of contributing to the guests' enjoyment of their holiday.

A typical day would begin with feeds at about 7.15 or 7.30 a.m., the duration obviously depending on the number of ponies. After breakfast, the ponies are groomed and tacked up ready for the morning ride, starting at about 10 a.m. The type of ride varies — some are with all novice riders, and will probably go out for a comparatively short time and return to the centre for lunch, while others may be out all day, with a halt en route for lunch. The staff left behind clean the yard, and prepare the hay and water for those ponies that are coming back at lunchtime. The afternoon ride (if there is one) would start at about 2.15 p.m. and last for, perhaps one and a half to two hours. On returning, the ponies must be unsaddled, and preparations made for the evening feed. Some ponies may be kept in, while others are turned out. This done, tack must be cleaned, and the yard swept, before finishing between 6.30 and 7 p.m.

Those are the bare essentials of a day's work, but employment in a trekking centre demands a great deal more than that. In their extremely useful and interesting circular *Guide to Pony Trekking and Holiday Riding*

Operators the Scottish Association recommends a number of points to which attention must be given if treks are to run smoothly, and many of these depend on the attitude and the responsibility of the ride leader or escort. For example they suggest that instructors should try to foster a happy atmosphere by being genial and polite at all times, and although that may seem obvious, it is something that should always be borne in mind. 'Good ride discipline is essential if accidents are to be avoided. This should be maintained by giving the riders clear and adequate instruction beforehand, and by the instructors being firm and decisive during rides. The instructors should know the countryside well enough to be able to point out things that will interest the riders. Landmarks, special views, historical or archeological sites and wild life should all be used to heighten the interest.' In this way, the instructors and trek leaders can add so much more to the guests' (and their own) interest in and enjoyment of the rides.

Hunt Service

The prospect of a career in hunt service has a great appeal to young men brought up in the hunting tradition, and for the ambitious and hard-working there are still good openings, with prospects of promotion probably better now than in days gone by.

A number of girls and young women are also attracted to hunt service, and some have succeeded in their ambition. In all fairness, however, it must be pointed out that there is a great deal more to the hunt servant's job than just galloping around the countryside on hunting days: there is also a great deal of very heavy and arduous work in the kennels which involves hauling, handling and skinning carcasses, lifting hounds when they need special attention, and a number of other jobs that are dirty and also require considerable physical strength. Many girls are really excellent in the hunting field, but while some *do* manage the kennel work, it is physically beyond many others.

Anyone wanting to enter hunt service must, of course, be able to ride well, and should not be too heavy. Masters are less than keen to provide expensive heavyweight horses for a hunt servant weighing upwards of twelve and a half stone! For the school leaver of sixteen to seventeen years of age, the first step should probably to be to work in some kind of stables for a year to gain experience. Then, ideally, he should obtain a position as stable staff in a hunt kennels, where he can learn the routine, and perhaps ride second horse to one of the hunt staff. In this way, he will be out hunting, and able to observe all that is going on. Other duties may include exercising hounds.

In the old days, the next rung up the ladder would normally have been an appointment as a second whipper-in. Today, only about half a dozen packs can afford the luxury of a second one, and young lads are thus 'thrown in at the deep end' as single-handed whippers-in, sometimes when they are only in their late teens or early twenties. In such a situation it is most desirable that the young hunt servant be with a good and understanding huntsman, and preferably in a small 'country'. Ambitions to go to one of the crack packs should be curbed until further experience has been gained.

The work of the young whipper-in varies according to the number of other staff kept, and also according to the time of the year. In general, hunt servants are occupied with hounds rather than with horses in their day-to-day work, and are usually (although not always these days) in the fortunate position of having their horses looked after for them by the stable staff.

The whipper-in's duties include cleaning the kennels and the hounds, preparing their food, including skinning carcasses and, in kennels where they cook, assisting with that. In early summer he is engaged in walking out hounds, and this usually involves coupling up the young hounds to the older ones. In a pack that has perhaps thirty or forty couple of youngsters, that can occupy an appreciable time. There is a great deal of work involved in breaking and making the young hounds before the start of cub-hunting in the autumn. During this period the young hunt servant should be taking the opportunity of acquiring a thorough knowledge of the hounds, learning all their names and building up a good relationship with them so that they will come to him readily at any time.

About June or July serious hound exercise begins, usually early in the morning to avoid the heat of the day. Initially, they are taken out for a short time, but this is gradually increased as they become fitter towards the start of the season. In some countries, this may involve five or six hours on the roads. It is important, too, that the young whipper-in devotes some of this time to learning the country over which he is going to hunt (assuming that he does not already know it). It is essential that he should develop 'an eye for a country'. Equally, he must take every opportunity to learn all he possibly can about foxes. He must have a sound knowledge of the run of a fox and the way it is likely to behave when disturbed, and be able to anticipate and tell his huntsman when hounds check which way the quarry has gone. This is an art that some take a very long time to acquire, but it is a necessary skill for the successful hunt servant.

When out hunting, the whipper-in's job is to keep a close eye on hounds, checking that all are present, and if they divide or get lost he must bring them back. He needs to study his huntsman's methods, as his principal task is to assist him as much as possible.

Promotion these days is probably quicker than it used to be, and a keen, efficient young hunt servant could expect to be first whipper-in to a good pack by the time he is twenty-three or twenty-four, and may be promoted to kennel-huntsman or huntsman by the age of about thirty. The kennel-huntsman has complete charge of hounds in kennels, directing their breaking and making, looking after the bitches when breeding, attending to illness and injury, in addition to understudying the master and taking over in the event of illness or injury. The huntsman also hunts hounds.

The job of a hunt servant is a skilled one, and it requires much more than just the ability to ride well. A good hunt servant must really be a countryman, with a love and feeling for the ways of the countryside, and an understanding of the behaviour of animals.

Young men seeking employment as hunt servants may contact the Masters of Foxhounds Association, Parsloes Cottage, Bagendon, Cirencester, Glos.

16 Courses of Further Education

At one time it would have been thought absurd to attend a university or technical college to learn about horses, but this, happily, is by no means the case now. Not only is it possible to obtain various certificates in horse and stable management at several agricultural or technical colleges, it is now possible to pursue a Master of Science course in Equine Studies at the University College of Wales at Aberystwyth.

Attending an institute of further education appeals to a number of people who, while wanting very much to work with horses, feel they would also like to enjoy the wider aspects of student life that attendance at a mixed-course college offers, and such courses perhaps offer a more academic approach than those at the majority of establishments catering for BHS, NPS or ABRS examinations. In addition, some include optional tuition in other skills such as secretarial studies. It should not, however, be concluded from these remarks, that the courses offered at colleges of higher education are in any way neglecting the practical aspect of their subjects − this is indeed not so − but the emphasis on actual *riding* will, in most cases, be very much less.

MSc Taught Courses in Equine Studies

At the top of the academic tree is the Master of Science Taught Course in Equine Studies at the University College of Wales at Aberystwyth, the only one of its kind in Europe and probably in the world. The course (which is comparatively new) was instituted because it was felt that, while the BHS and other bodies provided adequate vocational training for riding teachers, stud staff, etc., the horse has on the whole been neglected by scientists, other than from the veterinary angle, which by its very nature tends to concentrate on animals needing medical attention. There thus seemed to be scope for a course that dealt with the best means of managing *healthy* horses in all their aspects — nutrition, their performance as athletes, and general management — as well as related topics such as marketing, behavioural studies etc. The approach to these topics differs somewhat from the usual vocational course. In the latter, the emphasis tends to be on *how* things are done; at post-graduate level the emphasis is much more on *why*, and the students are encouraged throughout the course to be critical and analytical in their approach.

Enquiries showed great enthusiasm for a post-graduate course, and this enthusiasm is reflected in the fact that more than a hundred students apply for the eight to ten places available for each year's course. As the course is a post-graduate one, intending applicants must, of course, already hold a first degree, and this must be in a related subject such as physiology, agricultural science, zoology, etc. with first or second class honours. Candidates are also required to have had 'adequate pre-entry practical experience with horses'. This requirement is rather difficult to define, but each prospective candidate is interviewed and his or her experience assessed. It may for example, consist of possessing BHS, NPS, or ABRS qualifications, having been employed in a stud or riding school, or simply just having years of experience with the applicant's own animals.

The course (being a taught one as distinct from a purely research degree) consists of lectures, seminars and field work, and the preparation of a dissertation of not more than 20,000 words on a selected project that each student chooses in consultation with the lecturers. Four written papers are taken in June for the University Post-Graduate Diploma, and after acceptance and oral examination of the dissertation, the degree of Master of Science is awarded. The course covers one academic year, but an extra year may be taken in the preparation of the dissertation if this is deemed necessary.

Much of the field and practical work of the course is done at Llanarth Welsh Cob Stud, which was generously given to the University College some years ago by its founder, Miss Pauline Taylor, and her partner, Miss Lewis. This is of the greatest value, and some of the students are able to prepare their dissertations on research and investigations conducted at the stud. Not all the field studies are, however, conducted in Wales. Students go to Newmarket for about ten days, during which time they visit places of interest such as the Equine Research Station, the National Stud, go on rounds with some of the veterinary surgeons in the town, attend morning and evening stables at studs and racehorse training establishments, and go out on Newmarket Heath with trainers to learn about the training of racehorses.

During the university vacations students are found places at various establishments for two to four weeks, where they gain further practical experience, and wherever possible, devote time to areas of study connected with the subjects of their dissertations. In the past, students have been placed in various thoroughbred studs in Newmarket, at the National Foaling Bank, and in training yards. Not only do these vacation places contribute significantly towards the practical and academic content of the MSc course, they often introduce students to a number of people prominent in the field in which they hope to gain employment after obtaining their degrees.

The course itself is based on an advanced study of the following subjects:

1. Genetics and the horse. Methods of genetic improvement.
2. Anatomy and physiology of the horse.
3. Nutrition of the horse.
4. Breeding and stud management.

5. Behavioural studies.
6. The horse in health and disease.
7. Grassland and grazing management in relation to the horse.
8. Organisation, management and economics of horse enterprises and activities.

By the addition of supplementary courses the scheme is flexible enough to match the candidate's previous academic training and to meet the demands of the dissertation project. Supplementary courses are available in genetics, livestock improvement, feeds and feeding, applied physiology, animal health and hygiene, animal experimentation, and statistics.

Studies in genetics include the evolution and development of equines; chromosomes of the equine; qualitative and quantitative inheritance in the horse; heredity and environment – inheritance of fertility, growth and performance; breeding systems; selection methods; performance indices; premium stallion schemes; prediction of genetic value of stallions; efficiency of selection methods and improvement programmes; practical problems of attaining genetic improvement in the horse; colour inheritance; blood typing in horses.

Anatomy and physiology studies are concentrated on pre- and post-natal growth and development; body composition; nutritional and genetic influences on growth and development; factors affecting the attainment of sexual and physical maturity; the skeletal, muscular, respiratory, circulatory, nervous, endocrine, and reproductive systems; vision in the horse; dentition; the coat.

Equine structure and movement concentrates on conformation and performance; anatomy and physiology of the foot; corrective treatment; muscle structure and function; the physiology of exertion; muscular and haematological considerations; physiological tests of fitness.

Nutrition studies deal with the digestive system;

physiology of digestion and absorption; nutrient requirements of the pregnant and lactating mare; the nutrition of the foal; nutrient requirements for growth, maintenance and activity; symptoms of deficiency; dietary considerations; feeding systems; factors influencing voluntary feed intake.

Grassland and grazing management is studied in respect of the establishment and improvement of grassland on stud farms; suitable herbage species; paddock management and utilisation; the grazing behaviour and preferences of the horse; mineral availability; plant poisoning in horses.

Behavioural studies deal with learning, play behaviour, aggression; social organisation including reproductive and maternal behaviour in equines; vices, avoidance and control.

Breeding and stud management studies include the anatomy and physiology of reproduction in the mare and stallion; selection and rearing of colts; management of stallions; mating practices and performances; control of the oestrous cycle; pregnancy diagnosis; artificial insemination; foaling and lactation in brood mares; induction of parturition; adaptation of the foal to the extra-uterine environment; rearing practices; factors influencing the reproductive efficiency of the stud; replacement policies and systems.

The syllabus deals with the horse in health and disease, with emphasis on the inflammatory process and its control; the healing process and the management of wounds; control of disease and internal and external parasites in horses and ponies; common ailments; causes of infertility; nutritional disorders; causes of lameness; locating seat of lameness; repair of damaged tendons; respiratory disorders; infectious diseases; azoturia; equine sarcoids.

Organisation, management and economics of horse enterprises are studied with regard to the optimum use of farm or stud resources and facilities; opportunities and decision-making; socio-economic considerations; business management and financial controls; the economics of the working horse; the use of farm resources for ancillary horse enterprises; marketing; buildings, equipment and other facilities.

The role of the horse in the development of rural and urban society is also studied.

Field studies cover management and organisation of horse establishments; effective systems and methods of stable management; practical breeding plans; mating practices; conception rates and sire performances; stallion management and promotion; management of the mare and foal; maternal performance and suckling behaviour; care, treatment and handling of foals; considerations concerning castration of colt foals; feeding plans and methods; systems of pasture and grazing management; control of parasitism under grazing conditions; rearing methods and systems; replacement policies; learning, tractability and performance in young and mature horses; the assessment of performance and ability in horses; conformation and performance; conformation and soundness; care of the feet; first aid treatment of horses; buildings and equipment for horses; marketing; equipment; legislation; planning and organisation of horse activities.

The course authorities admit that people in the horse industry are still a little suspicious of graduates, and tend to think that they may have their heads full of theory, with little practical experience. Undoubtedly the syllabus *does* contain an impressive amount of theory, but this is fully backed up by plenty of practical work, and as more students graduate from the course, so will the horse world appreciate their true worth. Past students have already obtained some excellent positions. Some are on the staff of colleges of further education, lecturing and demonstrating in horse stud and stable management courses; one has returned to her native America and holds an excellent post working with Quarter Horses;

another hopes to work towards managing a Thorough-bed stud, while yet another plans to obtain a research post in one of the equine foodstuff firms. For the scientifically-minded horseman or horsewoman, this course is particularly attractive, although with so few places available, no one should set their hearts on doing it to the exclusion of all else.

Warwickshire College of Agriculture

The Warwickshire College of Agriculture offers a two-year full-time residential course leading to the Diploma in Horse Management, and a one-year certificate course in Horse Management on Farms and Estates.

The objective of the diploma course is to produce a person with sufficient background knowledge and practical skill to enable him or her to carry out the majority of day-to-day tasks associated with stable and stud management and the related farming enterprises, and to be able to keep and process the relevant records and accounts. At the end of the course participants should be capable of employing a large range of planning skills in a variety of horse and relevant agricultural situations, and after a further period of practical experience should be capable of taking full responsibility for a horse enterprise. Most holders of the diploma look forward eventually to obtaining good management posts in various sections of the horse world, but initially they are more likely to find posts as head girls or lads on studs, or as assistant stud managers or assistant stud grooms while gaining further experience. Past students have obtained positions of some responsibility on the organisational and showing sides of studs, in riding schools and, in one instance, in arranging the transport of horses by sea and air.

Prospective students must be at least seventeen and a half years of age on 1st September in the year of entry to the course; have four GCE 'O' levels (or equivalent) including English language and one science subject, or the college entry examination; have adequate and appropriate practical experience of working with horses for a minimum of one year full time; have one of the following certificates (or provide evidence that their riding and stable management ability is of equivalent standard or better); BHS Certificate of Horsemastership, Irish Certificate in Equitation Science, BHS Horse Knowledge and Riding Certificate 3rd Stage, Pony Club 'B' Standard Test, BHS Riding Club Grade III Test, or NPS Certificate in Pony Mastership and Breeding for Stud Assistants (non-riding). Final selection depends on a personal interview with the principal when candidates are expected to exhibit determination and enthusiasm to follow a career in the management of horses.

The syllabus is taught by means of a series of lectures, seminars, tutorials, laboratory and post-mortem work, practical work including individual projects, industrial experience, and educational tours and visits.

The college has its own stud of Welsh Section D cobs, the present stallion being Llanarth bred. The idea behind this is to have a nucleus of purebred cobs, whose temperaments make them ideal for students to work with, learning in-hand show production, driving, and producing for ridden classes. They are also keeping a number of the young stock for breeding purposes to show, for instance, line-breeding, and to bring on as general-purpose performance animals. The cobs have been shown successfully at the Royal Welsh and the Northleach shows. The stud also has a number of Thoroughbreds, because everything connected with the horse side of the college is required to be a commercially viable venture, and it was felt desirable to produce horses for eventing, dressage, etc., and, particularly in the good hunter area which surrounds the college, hunters. A breeding programme of crossing the Section Ds with the Thoroughbreds was undertaken, but it has been found that the animals produced were

too small, so the stud is now planning to cross their
Thoroughbreds with Irish draught horses, Cleveland
Bays, or Hanovarians.

The college also runs a livery yard specialising in the
breaking and schooling of young horses, and the re-
schooling of problem animals, with the students being
fully involved. The greater part of the work is done 'from
the ground', by lungeing, long-reining, and loose schooling, and the approach is, as might be expected from such
an institution, along scientific lines. The students are
taught anatomy and the structure and functions of
muscles in some detail, and this is put to particular use
in the breaking and schooling. The horse is developed as
an athlete, and before any schooling is done, a series of
measurements is taken to determine any deviation such
as curvature of the spine, atrophy of muscles, or in-
equality of muscular development. The aim is to produce
the horse so that it can perform to its full potential, and
this is done with special regard to muscle development,
producing the correct muscles for weight carrying, for
freedom of shoulder movement and encouraging the
maximum thrust and transmission of energy from behind.

More time than usual in most breaking yards is spent
on the work from the ground, but the course tutors are
convinced of its worth in the long term, as they aim to
eliminate all the evasions etc. before the horse ever has
a rider on its back. The students carry out the schooling,
but *always* under supervision. With a sound basis of
anatomy, they are able to analyse the horse's movements,
and learn to tell at a glance what muscle groups are
involved, where a problem originates, and why a particular
evasion occurs. Every horse that comes for breaking or
schooling is analysed and discussed with the aid of photo-
graphs and films. Once broken and backed, the horses
go back to their owners, but are frequently returned to
the college for secondary schooling.

During the course, students attend a day a week at a
nearby nationally known riding academy, not to receive

riding instruction but to see competition horses being schooled and to take part in the training programmes. The whole emphasis of this part of the course is on teaching the students how to produce horses for the various fields in which they are to compete. In the future it is hoped to take in horses, particularly Arabs, and produce them for racing, and to develop some training programmes for other disciplines, such as long-distance riding.

The course works very closely with two veterinary surgeons, one from an equine practice and one from a general practice, and they deal with veterinary health, breeding problems, etc. The owner of one of the country's best known Arabian studs also lectures on such topics as the practical running of a stud, registration, breeds, breed crosses, use of the Arab and its influence on ponies, and the history of the Arabian breed. Grassland management, animal production, crop husbandry, estate management, and management of associated topics are taught by the agricultural staff of the college.

The horse sections of the syllabus for the first year of the diploma course include: description of the horse, the skeleton, lower limbs, feet, skeletal conformation, ideal proportions, with appropriate demonstrations, practical dissections and discussions; genetics; breeding programmes and associated topics, with visits to see prepotent stallions and their progeny; anatomy and physiology with particular reference to the horse, including examination and dissection of various systems; stable management in all its aspects; maintenance of riding standards and instruction in how to recognise and assess potential in the horse; lungeing, behaviour, the senses, vices, saddlery, bits, ancillary devices, lungeing and long-reining equipment; thorough instruction in the theory and practice of nutrition in the horse; the principles of grassland management in relation to a horse enterprise; knowledge and understanding of the various disorders of the horse, their cause, prevention and treatment; a basic understanding of business techniques and related matters.

In the second year, students learn to assess the conformation of the horse and to use this assessment beneficially; stable planning and design, safety and hygiene; the training of horses, psychology in training; training foals, yearlings, etc., corrective work, backing, riding away, harness work, driving vehicles, lungeing, principles and practice of long-reining, in-hand work, loose schooling, fitness training and exercise, methods of training; further veterinary studies; relation of principles of horse and staff management to the day to day running of a horse unit; knowledge of the principles and practice of horse breeding and stud management.

Throughout, visits are made to a wide variety of horse enterprises to give students a wide knowledge of the various facets of the horse industry.

The one-year certificate course is also residential. It is a practical-based course intended for those who see their future in the day-to-day operation of a horse enterprise. It provides an opportunity to learn something of the art and staff management to the day-to-day running of a the relationship of horses to land use.

To this end the course includes some agriculture, particularly those aspects which may sometimes be associated with a horse enterprise. These include beef and sheep production systems, calf rearing and grassland management. The equine part of the syllabus looks in some detail at the care of the horse, as well as covering stable and stud management.

Other aspects of the course include some instruction and practice in the elementary skills required to maintain a stable yard in good order, basic driving skills and routine maintenance of the farm tractor and an appreciation of elementary office routines and accounting systems.

Acceptance for the course is dependent on the candidate being at least seventeen and a half years old, having had at least one year full-time working with horses, having had a good general education up to GCE 'O' level standard (or equivalent) and providing evidence that his/her riding and stable management ability is of a suitable standard.

Further details may be obtained from the Warwickshire College of Agriculture, Moreton Hall, Moreton Morrell, Warwicks, CV35 9BL.

West Oxfordshire College

The West Oxfordshire Technical College offers a one-year full-time course in Stud and Stable Husbandry which is very much orientated towards the racing and Thoroughbred stud industry. This is emphasised by the composition of the course's Academic Advisory Board, whose members include a representative of the National Trainers' Association and a member of the Thoroughbred Breeders' Association. The course tutor is reluctant to accept students who are not aiming in that direction, as he considers that while there are plenty of *jobs* available in other branches of the horse world, the racing and Thoroughbred stud industry offers much more opportunity for *careers,* with better remuneration and prospects of promotion. The course tutor has excellent contacts within the industry, and at the time of writing, all the previous year's employable students had positions to go to a month before they finished at the college.

For entry to the course, students must have three GCE 'O' levels or CSE Grade 1 equivalents, and be at least seventeen years of age. A minimum of one year's practical experience with horses is required, but there is some flexibility about this, as it is recognised that experience with horses frequently begins before leaving school. The relevance and depth of this experience and its demonstration of a definite career intention are all taken into account when allocating places. All British applicants are interviewed, and are asked to ride. Although no equitation instruction is given (and it is in no way a riding course) students must be able to ride well enough to take part in breaking and schooling young horses.

The course is a comprehensive one, and undertakes the study of horse management in its widest sense. Thus not only do the students study all aspects of stud and stable management, they are also required to take the City and Guilds of London Agriculture Phase I and Grassland, Forage and Feed Cereals Phase II examinations. Considerable importance is attached to the farming aspects, as it is felt that prospective management staff must, for example, understand the problems of cereal-growing to enable them to buy foodstuffs efficiently, and be familiar with beef production because it is difficult to manage land satisfactorily without an alternative form of livestock. The Oxfordshire Local Authority has a large teaching farm, and the Stud and Stable Husbandry course has a corner of this with a dairy herd, pigs, grassland and cereals, where students are taught the practical aspects of farming. On the administrative side of both farming and horse management, accounts and records are studied, as the tutor believes that one of the greatest weaknesses in the horse industry is poor accounting and costing. Students are very much involved with the financial side of the animals as well as working with them.

Although approximately two-thirds of the course is theoretical, valuable practical experience is gained with the co-operation of local riding centres and Thoroughbred studs, including that belonging to the course tutor. The first three weeks of the course are spent almost entirely on practical work, so that all may reach approximately the same standard before proceeding further. The students are given a schedule of practical tasks involving both the equine and the general farming sections of the syllabus, which must be undertaken during the year. They are expected to reach experienced worker standard in these practical skills, and must complete a written record sheet noting the most important points of each.

At the end of the course they may be asked to demonstrate their competence in any of the skills acquired. The tasks range from simple routine skills such as mucking out and demonstrating the management of a straw bed, to more specialised knowledge such as describing the circumstances in which help should be given to a mare at foaling. On the farming side, they must, for instance, assess and report on the physical conditions of at least three soil samples, and measure out or estimate the quantities of bulk and concentrate food needed for a specified group of yarded cattle.

During the year all students work (two at a time) for ten days to a fortnight at a nearby Thoroughbred stud, where they learn stud routine, organisation of teasing and service, mare and foal handling, and they are expected to be on call twenty-four hours a day during the foaling season. At another Thoroughbred stud they learn about mare and foal management, and yearling sale preparation, and they actually prepare the stud's yearlings for sale. Practical experience in the various listed tasks is gained at yet another stud, clipping is done at two local riding centres, and difficult horses are handled at a long-distance riding centre. In all, some 300 horses are available.

The students also go on a series of educational visits. Among the trainers' yards visited is one with a solarium and another with a swimming pool; the students also visit the Newmarket and the Lambourn Gallops and learn about their organisation; they visit Tattersalls, the Doncaster and Ascot Sales, Newbury Racecourse, and three famous Thoroughbred studs.

In addition to the compulsory sections of the syllabus, students may also take typing and shorthand, instruction in the use of extra machinery, farm business management, or enterprise operation and control. At the end of the course, successful students obtain a certificate in Horse Management from the college, plus certificates in Agriculture, Grassland, and Accounts and Records from the City and Guilds of London Institute; and a certificate in first aid from the St John Ambulance. The acquisition of all these certificates entitles the student to the college certificate in Stud and Stable Husbandry.

The syllabus includes the following topics: explanation of the broad climatic, topographic, soil, farm and population factors which influence horse enterprises; explanation of the economic and social importance of horse enterprises; structure and function with emphasis on the body form and function, bone, muscle and fat; the layout and purpose of the digestive, respiratory, circulatory, excretory and mammary systems; elements of farriery, including recognition of all types of shoe, plate, nails, pads, studs and tools in common use, lameness, blistering and firing; nutrition, health and disease; reproduction and breeding, including the principles of inheritance, the commercially important characteristics of mares, teasing methods, organisation of service including pre-service disease control, requirements of a foaling box, stages of parturition, routine checks on newborn foal, symptoms and treatment of meconium retention, normal disease precautions in case of newborn foal, methods of dealing with an orphan foal, mare and foal management to weaning including the use of a foal creep, methods of weaning including their advantages and disadvantages, management of the weanling and yearling; exercise, including the advantages and disadvantages of a horsewalker and of swimming horses; breaking, with practical knowledge of lungeing, long-reining, backing, and riding the young horse; vices: the identification of the cause and its control where possible; housing: the normal housing requirements for all classes of stock, with advantages and disadvantages of the systems commercially available: grooming: the aims and different methods available; saddlery, harness and clothing; transport, including advantages and disadvantages of the forms available, preparing a horse for transport, methods of dealing with awkward loaders, travelling a horse abroad; selling and sales: presenting a horse for sale, duties to

owner, dealing with enquiries from prospective pur-
chasers, conditions of sale used by most auctioneers,
normal procedures for veterinary examination of horses
for sale; insurance: explanation and examples of rates
for and conditions of insurance for stallions, brood mares,
flat racers, yearlings, foals, hurdlers, steeplechasers,
show horses, hacks, drivers, hunters and eventers, brood
mares against barrenness, prospective foal, stallion infertility, temporary transit; rules of racing and General
Stud Book regulations.

Also included is the City and Guilds of London
Agriculture Phase 1 which covers the farm tractor,
machine elements and hand tools, the soil and the plant,
animal feeding and rearing, livestock and crop production. The City and Guilds Phase 2 includes cereals
and combinable break crops, grassland, forage and feed
cereal crops, farm accounts and records, beef production.

Useful Addresses

ASSOCIATION OF BRITISH RIDING SCHOOLS,
7 Deer Park Road,
Sawtry,
Huntingdon,
Cambridgeshire PE17 5TT

BRITISH HORSE SOCIETY,
British Equestrian Centre,
Kenilworth,
Warwickshire CV8 2LR

BRITISH SHOW JUMPING ASSOCIATION,
British Equestrian Centre,
Kenilworth,
Warwickshire CV8 2LR

CORDWAINERS' TECHNICAL COLLEGE,
Mare Street,
Hackney,
London E8 3RE

COUNCIL FOR SMALL INDUSTRIES IN RURAL AREAS
(CoSIRA),
35 Camp Road,
Wimbledon Common,
London SW19 4UP

ENGLISH RIDING HOLIDAY AND TREKKING ASSOCIATION,
c/o Approvals Office,
British Horse Society,
British Equestrian Centre,
Kenilworth,
Warwickshire CV8 2LR

HEREFORDSHIRE TECHNICAL COLLEGE,
Folly Lane,
Hereford HR1 1LS

HOUSEHOLD CAVALRY REGIMENT,
Hyde Park Barracks,
Knightsbridge,
London SW7

MASTER OF FOXHOUNDS ASSOCIATION,
Parsloes Cottage,
Bagendon,
Cirencester,
Gloucestershire

METROPOLITAN POLICE,
Mounted Branch,
Imber Court,
East Molesey,
Surrey

NATIONAL FARRIERS', BLACKSMITHS' AND
AGRICULTURAL ENGINEERS' ASSOCIATION,
674 Leeds Road,
Lofthouse Gate,
Wakefield WF3 3HJ

NATIONAL PONY SOCIETY,
7 Cross and Pillory Lane,
Alton,
Hampshire

NATIONAL TRAINERS' FEDERATION,
42 Portman Square,
London W1H 0AP

PONY TREKKING AND RIDING SOCIETY OF WALES,
Tudor Cottage,
Llwyndafydd,
Llandysul,
Dyfed SA44 6LD

ROYAL COLLEGE OF VETERINARY SURGEONS,
32 Belgrave Square,
London SW1X 8QP

ROYAL HORSE ARTILLERY,
The King's Troup,
Ordnance Hill,
St John's Wood,
London NW8 6PT

SCOTTISH TREKKING AND RIDING ASSOCIATION,
Tomnacairn Farm,
Trochry,
Dunkeld,
Perthshire

SOCIETY OF MASTER SADDLERS,
9 St Thomas Street,
London SE1

UNIVERSITY COLLEGE OF WALES,
Aberystwyth,
Dyfed

WARWICKSHIRE COLLEGE OF AGRICULTURE,
Moreton Hall,
Moreton Morrell,
Warwickshire CV35 9BL

WEST OXFORDSHIRE TECHNICAL COLLEGE,
Holloway Road,
Witney,
Oxfordshire

WORSHIPFUL COMPANY OF FARRIERS,
3 Hamilton Road,
Cockfosters,
Barnet,
Hertfordshire

Index